TV Newscast
Processes and Procedures

Multiple Camera Video Series

By Robert J. Schihl

Television Commercial Processes and Procedures

Talk Show and Entertainment Program Processes and Procedures

Studio Drama Processes and Procedures

TV Newscast Processes and Procedures

TV Newscast
Processes and Procedures

Robert J. Schihl, Ph.D.

Focal Press

Boston London

Focal Press is an imprint of Butterworth–Heinemann.

Recognizing the importance of preserving what has been
written, it is the policy of Butterworth–Heinemann to have the
books it publishes printed on acid-free paper, and we exert our
best efforts to that end.

Library of Congress Cataloging-in-Publication Data

Schihl, Robert J.
    TV newscast processes and procedures / Robert J.
Schihl.
    p.   cm.—(Multiple camera video series)
Includes bibliographical references (p.   ) and index.
ISBN 0-240-80094-X (pbk.)
    1. Television broadcasting of news.   2. Television—
Production and direction.   I. Title.   II. Series: Schihl,
Robert J.   Multiple camera video series.
PN4784.T4S295   1991
070.1'95—dc20   91-16862
                                                     CIP

British Library Cataloguing in Publication Data

Schihl, Robert J.
    TV newscast processes and procedures.—
(Multiple camera video series)
I. Title II. Series
070.195

    ISBN 0-240-80094-X

Butterworth–Heinemann
80 Montvale Avenue
Stoneham, MA 02180

10 9 8 7 6 5 4 3 2 1

Printed in the United States of America

Contents

Chapter 4   Description and Glossary for Studio Production Organizing Forms / 113

Preface

Multiple camera video production refers to those varying video projects that create the products of the multiple camera video technology. It is usually the video production associated with a studio setting. Some of the most common multiple camera studio production today includes newscast production, drama production (mainly soap operas), talk show/entertainment production, and television commercial production. Of these, only the daily newscast and occasional television commercial are still being produced at local television production studios. Occasionally, public service talk shows are produced at the local facility.

In network television studio production, besides the daily newscasts, the continuing daily soap opera production still occupies one of the busiest and most productive of the studio projects.

While the basic skills necessary for studio production remain the same across studio production genres, preproduction tasks and production roles vary immensely from one genre to another. The beginning television producer, director, and production crews need to be aware of those studio production elements that are similar across genres as well as those that differ. It is not uncommon to find well-meaning beginners performing poorly in their roles across genres when principles and criteria for one genre were erroneously applied to another. Professionally, even apparently similar studio production roles across television program genres require a different mind set and, consequently, different skills application. Hence, at beginning and intermediate television production levels, awareness of the various genres and their differences encourages varying skill development and consequent employment marketability.

Academic goals for beginning television production skills are usually oriented to some form of studio operation. Therein students have the opportunity to learn all aspects of video production from the technology of the medium to the aesthetics of the final product. In some academic programs, knowledge of these concepts and skills is required before advancing to the single camera video experience. The television studio experience encompasses all phases of video *producing skills* from those of the producer to those of the director and all phases of video *production technology* from that of the camera operator (video camera skills) to that of the technical director (video editing skills). Given success in the learning stages of video production, skills still need expression. The most common expression of video production skills is to engage in some form of television studio production. Beyond a basic television studio production handbook, there is not an adequate text available to design and organize differing studio production genres. This book concentrates on producing and the production of the television studio newscast.

The growth of both broadcast and cable television in the United States and abroad in the 1990s shows ever increasing development and expansion. The areas of low power television (LPTV) production, the continuing increase in cable origination programming, and the introduction of high definition television (HDTV) attest to that development and expansion. The rapid fragmentation of cable and satellite television in general is spurring the proliferation of independent television production facilities and the multiplication of television studio program genres. Producers for these independently produced and syndicated programs seek from media conventions the guidelines for producing and the production of the various genres. Publishers of books on the subject of television are seeing a growing need in these areas and are responding with an increasing number of publications. These publications assist the entrepreneur in the development of video production houses and in the training of producers. What is needed by both the broadcast educator as well as the video production entrepreneur is guidance for producing and production procedures, information on video production organizational flow, and the definition of video producing and production roles.

Following the publication of my earlier book *Single Camera Video: From Concept to Edited Master* (Focal Press, 1989), I found that educators, beginning professionals, and industry reviewers alike applauded the format in which I presented the procedural, organizational, and role definition stages of the single camera video technology. I was asked why such a format was not available for multiple camera video production. Having spent more years both in broadcast education and professional production with multiple camera video production than with single camera video production, I asked myself the same question. I hope this text is the desired response.

TV Newscast Processes and Procedures is intended to meet the needs of those individuals from intermediate television education to the beginning television production facility entrepreneur who needs a clear and comprehensive road map to organizing a television studio newscast production. This book presents the conceptual preproduction stages of program production (e.g., news production budget, news set design, and newscast format design) as well as all levels of production skill definition and organization until the studio director and news producer call for a wrap to the studio production. This road map includes the thoroughness of flowcharts for all preproduction, production, and (when it should be necessary) postproduction personnel roles and the specific detail of preproduction and production organizing forms that facilitate and expedite most roles throughout the process of the studio production of a television newscast.

In *Single Camera Video: From Concept to Edited Master* I referred to the approach I took as "a cookbook recipe approach." I have not only not regretted the comparison but have grown confirmed in the analogy. Similar to single camera video production, multiple camera video production is a process needing the guidance of a good kitchen recipe—an ordered, procedural, and detailed set of guidelines. As with a good recipe, after initial success, a good cook adjusts ingredients, eliminates some, adds others, and makes substitutions according to taste and experience with the recipe. So, too, is it with the approach taken in this text. The production organizing details covered in this text are such that after initial introduction, depending often on available personnel, studio equipment, or production time frame, preproduction and production task roles can be multiplied, combined, or eliminated—just like the ingredients in a favorite recipe.

Specifically, the approach that this text takes to multiple camera video production is one of organization. The most frequent and vociferous compliment to *Single Camera Video* is that it organizes the whole gamut of the preproduction, production, and postproduction of single camera video production. In the same way, this text is designed to organize the multiple camera video production of the newscast. This text concentrates on the most common television studio production genre: the television newscast. Books on the other television studio genres (the talk show/entertainment program, the television studio drama production, and the television studio commercial production) are also available from Focal Press in worktexts similar to this.

The process of television newscast production is presented in Chapter 1 in flowchart checklist form for preproduction, production, and postproduction stages of production. For each of the three stages, producing and production personnel roles are presented, with responsibilities and obligations listed in their order of accomplishment. In Chapter 2, the processes of preproduction, production, and postproduction are presented in chronological order of production role performance. In Chapter 3, production organization forms are provided for various preproduction and production tasks. These forms are designed to facilitate the goal or producing and production requirements at certain stages of the process of producing and production. A description of and glossary for each form are presented in Chapter 4 to facilitate use of the forms.

In determining the method of presenting the television newscast production genre in this text, some choices had to be made. Production procedures had to be adapted to a learning process. The first choice was to decide the number of producing personnel and the studio production crew size. The number of producing roles and studio production crew members usually is determined by the production budget and the number of available personnel (i.e., students) in an academic environment. The choice was made to create above-the-line and below-the-line staff and crew for an average size production with a minimum number of personnel. As in the analogy of a good recipe, combine, subtract, or multiply staff and crew members according to costs and availability. The industry does that, too.

Another choice was to determine the level of studio hardware and technology sophistication to assume in newscast production. No two television studio facilities are alike, especially in academic environments. The criterion for level of hardware and technology sophistication assumed was to be aware that no matter how much or how little a studio facility has in terms of hardware and technology, the students leaving their training time in any type of production facility still have to know some point of minimal reference to the "real world" of newscast production and employment skill expectation standards. A teacher of broadcasting can easily structure this text and its approach to an individual facility. Without an ideal point of reference, it would be very difficult to structure up to a level that was not covered in this text. Students must be made aware of what to expect in a "normal" or "ideal" newscast production facility and from a newscast production crew. This is what I have tried to convey. I have taught news production from a minimal facility to a full blown state-of-the-art facility. This text is adaptable to either.

I repeat what I wrote in *Single Camera Video*. The video production industry or television newscast production is not standardized in the procedural manner in which its video products are created. This text, although it can appear to recommend standardized approaches to achieving video products, is not intended to imply that the industry or news production is standardized nor is it an attempt to standardize the industry or news production. The presentation of ordered production steps is merely academic; it is a way of teaching and learning required stages in video production. The video product is the result of a creative process and should remain that way. This text provides order and organization to television newscast production for beginning producers and directors and for intermediate television teachers and students of video production. Once someone becomes familiar with the process of any television newscast production, that person is encouraged to use what works and facilitates a task and to drop or rethink those elements that do not work or no longer facilitate the task.

I am currently a full professor—both a charter and senior television faculty member—at Regent University on the grounds of the Christian Broadcasting Network, home of the Family Channel. I teach in both the School of Radio, Television, and Film, and the School of Journalism.

A.M.D.G.
Robert J. Schihl, Ph.D.
Virginia Beach, Virginia
1991

ACKNOWLEDGMENTS

I am indebted to many people over many years who have contributed unknowingly to this book:

To Joanne, Joel, and Jonathan for putting up with the interminable clacking of computer keys and the whine of a printer;

To my parents, Harold and Lucille, who unwittingly turned me on to television production in 1950 by purchasing our first television set;

To Dr. Marilyn Stahlka Watt, Chair, Department of Communication, Canisius College, Buffalo, New York, for introducing me to television broadcasting and the talk show genre, and for making me a television producer;

To Edward Herbert and Kurt Eichsteadt, Taft Broadcasting, for giving me the chance to have my own live, local prime-time television program;

To Marion P. Robertson, Chief Executive Officer, the Family Channel, Virginia Beach, Virginia, for giving me the opportunity to work and teach in a state-of-the-art national network television facility;

To Dean David Clark, Provost George Selig, and President Bob Slosser, Regent University, Virginia Beach, Virginia, for granting me the sabbatical to write this book;

To Karen Speerstra, Senior Editor, and Philip Sutherland, Acquisitions Editor, Focal Press, Stoneham, Massachusetts, for being the most encouraging editors and friends an author could have;

To Rob Cody, Project Manager; Julie Blim, "700 Club" Producer; and John Loiseides, Photographer, Christian Broadcasting Network, Virginia Beach, Virginia, for their research assistance;

To my thousands of television students from the State University of New York at Buffalo, the State University of New York College at Buffalo, Hampton University, and Regent University, and especially to those among them whose names I see regularly on the closing credits of network and affiliate television programs—for the thrill of seeing their names.

Key to the Book

Creating a successful television studio production requires that many tasks at varying stages of production be performed in sequential order. Most tasks build upon one another and are interrelated with the tasks of other production personnel. The television industry has clearly defined roles for each production personnel member. This book provides a blueprint of the duties assigned to each production role. The duties of each role—producer, director, camera operator, etc.—are first presented in a checklist flowchart. Role duties are then cross-referenced within the text on the basis of studio production stages. The tasks necessary for every production role are divided and arranged at each stage of the production process. The flowchart is divided into the three chronological stages of television studio production: preproduction, production, and postproduction.

This book can be used as a text or reference. The reader can gain a comprehensive understanding of the production process by reading the entire book. The reader also can check specific personnel responsibilities or use particular forms.

Chapter 1 presents a flowchart for preproduction, production, and postproduction stages by personnel role and in sequential task order (see figure).

Chapter 2 details each production task in the order in which it is to be completed.

Chapter 3 provides production organizing forms.

Chapter 4 is a key to terms and information for the production forms in Chapter 3.

Following is a listing of the personnel abbreviations used throughout this text.

Personnel	Abbreviation
News director	ND
Executive producer	EP
Assignment editor	AE
News producer	NP
Talent	T
Editorialist	E
Reporters/writers	R/W
Feature producer	FP
Graphic artist/producer	G
Script editor	SE
Videographer	VG
Video editor	VE
Studio director	D
Assistant director	AD
Technical director	TD
Production assistant	PA
Audio director	A
Floor director	F
Studio camera operators	CO
Teleprompter operator	TO
Telecine operator	TC
Lighting director	LD
Videotape recorder operator	VTRO
Video engineer	VEG

Choose a television studio production stage. Here, the PREPRODUCTION stage was chosen.

Each television studio production role is abbreviated (e.g., P) and sequential production tasks numbered (e.g., (1), (2), (3), etc.). To locate the third PREPRODUCTION task responsibility of a PRODUCER (P) look down the checklist for (3).

Every television studio production role and task is listed here and is explained in detail in Chapter 2. The page number after the entry directs you to the explanation. Chapter 2 will also aid you in learning the responsibilities of the other crew members.

Reading this information will indicate if there is a production organizing form available in Chapter 3 to assist you in a particular task.

Each television studio production organizing form is explained in detail in a glossary of terms and information required for the form in Chapter 4.

PREPRODUCTION

PRODUCER (P)

☐ (1) Hires/chooses newscast producing/production personnel **15**
☐ (2) Keeps the budget; authorizes expenses (production budget form) **15**
☐ (3) Designs/decides the studio news set (news set design form) **15**
☐ (4) Designs/decides newscast production values (newscast design form) **15**
☐ (5) Creates/maintains the newscast format (newscast format form) **16**
☐ (6) Auditions/chooses talent/editorialist (talent audition form) **16**
☐ (7) Chairs the newscast planning conference for each newscast **20**
☐ (8) Is responsible for newscast philosophy, policy, news judgments, etc. **23**
☐ (9) Oversees the choice of an editorial **23**
☐ (10) Oversees the production of all newscasts; keeps newscast on the air **25**
☐ (11) Edits/approves editorial **28**
☐ (12) Functions as managing editor **28**
☐ (13) Reviews/critiques newscasts with personnel **37**

Chapter 1

Television Newscast Production

INTRODUCTION

The most omnipresent genre of television programming in the United States is the television news program. In virtually every television broadcast market across the country, there are usually three locally originated television newscasts. Each of the three local newscasts is probably an affiliate of one of the three network television corporations—ABC, CBS, or NBC. The importance of the local television newscasts stands as a measure of the share of each local affiliate's viewing audience. The ratings data generated during ratings sweep periods on the 6:00 and 11:00 newscasts of the affiliate stations determine the ranking in the market of the standing of each of the network affiliates. In some markets, the newscasts are the only local origination television programming produced by each television station. The job success and security of station personnel from anchor to news director rise or fall with the ratings results. The largest budget within most local television stations is for the support of the newscast; successes in commercial sales are a function of the ranking of the newscasts in a market after ratings. The most marketable experience for graduates with degrees from academic programs in television production and electronic journalism is television newscast production. The most likely first employment opportunity for experienced graduates probably will be with local television news departments. For these reasons, understanding the organization, producing, and production processes of the television newscast is most important to broadcast educators and beginning professionals.

Throughout the 1980s and into the 1990s, television news continues to enjoy exposure and success unlike any it has ever known. In the history of television broadcasting and cablecasting, there has never been such a breadth of newscast viewing choices, news diversification, or news saturation. Skepticism greeted the rise of Turner Broadcasting System's 24-hour newscasts. That skepticism soon turned to admiration and imitation. By 1990 there were no less than seven national, early evening television newscasts: ABC's "The ABC World News Tonight," CBS's "The CBS Evening News," NBC's "The NBC Nightly News," CNN's "Headline News," CNN's "The World Today," PBS's "MacNeil-Lehrer Newshour," and the Discovery Channel's "World Monitor." Besides these network newscasts, there is the proliferation of specialized newscasts such as "Entertainment Tonight" for news from the show business world, "The World Business Report" for news from the world of economics, the Family Channel's "NewSight" for international religious news, as well as the full-time channels of specialized news, including the Weather Channel, ESPN (the sports channel), and even C-Span for news from the government. There appears to be no end in sight for the proliferation of newscasts as well. Ratings data concur: There is no dearth of audience for news and newscasts. It would seem to be in the interest of beginning professionals both within and outside academia to study the design, process, and organization of newscast production.

FLOWCHART AND CHECKLIST

Many aspects of most technologies imply an ordered and procedural manner to task accomplishment. This is especially true of television production in general and television studio newscast production in particular. In the area of news producing (news preproduction)—from newscast design to the format/rundown sheet—there is a clear temporal priority to most tasks. Some tasks definitely must be accomplished before succeeding tasks can be begun. In the studio, newscast production demands a priority of task accomplishment before videotaping can begin. The format of a newscast is the expression of order and procedure.

Following is a flowchart and checklist of preproduction, production, and postproduction steps in television newscast producing and production. These steps are presented in *chronological order* of accomplishment by producing and production role responsibilities. The abbreviation codes following role titles in the checklist correlate to the *production order* of these roles described in Chapter 2, which details the processes of newscast production.

As producing and production tasks are accomplished, a check mark can be placed in the box preceding each task as a visual cue to the steps accomplished and those yet to be completed. The checklist is an excellent log for the individual crew and supervisory personnel as a record of stages of producing and production and a record of learning achieved.

FLOWCHART AND CHECKLIST FOR NEWSCAST PRODUCTION

PREPRODUCTION	PRODUCTION	POSTPRODUCTION
NEWS DIRECTOR (ND)	**NEWS DIRECTOR (ND)**	**NEWS DIRECTOR (ND)**
☐ (1) Hires/chooses newscast producing/production personnel **15**	☐ (1) Makes a last minute check with the studio director and newscast talent **39**	(If the newscast just produced is a tape-delayed telecast, some postproduction may be undertaken. If so, the news director may be involved.)
☐ (2) Keeps the budget; authorizes expenses (production budget form) **15**	☐ (2) Monitors the newscast from the staff office/newsroom area **39**	☐ (1) May assume some responsibility/decision-making role to add or redo elements of the newscast **51**
☐ (3) Designs/decides the studio news set (news set design form) **15**		☐ (2) Communicates those elements of the newscast producing stage that will be a part of the postproduction **51**
☐ (4) Designs/decides newscast production values (newscast design form) **15**		☐ (3) Continues as in the production stage **51**
☐ (5) Creates/maintains the newscast format (newscast format form) **16**		
☐ (6) Auditions/chooses talent/editorialist (talent audition form) **16**		
☐ (7) Chairs the newscast planning conference for each newscast **20**		
☐ (8) Is responsible for newscast philosophy, policy, news judgments, etc. **23**		
☐ (9) Oversees the choice of an editorial **23**		
☐ (10) Oversees the production of all newscasts; keeps newscast on the air **25**		
☐ (11) Edits/approves editorial **28**		
☐ (12) Functions as managing editor **28**		
☐ (13) Reviews/critiques newscasts with personnel **37**		
EXECUTIVE PRODUCER (EP) (or ASSISTANT NEWS DIRECTOR)		
☐ (1) Manages the newsroom, news personnel, news gathering sources **16**		
☐ (2) Is responsible for individual newscasts/day-by-day details **16**		
☐ (3) Creates individual newscast formats, content, and order (newscast format form) **16**		
☐ (4) Attends newscast planning conference **21**		
☐ (5) Oversees program producers **25**		
☐ (6) Makes continuing format decisions/changes throughout the day **26**		
☐ (7) Reports to/communicates with the news director throughout the day **26**		
ASSIGNMENT EDITOR (AE)		
☐ (1) Keeps up on/aware of news makers, events, and potential news **16**		
☐ (2) Assigns news stories; keeps assignment board updated (newscast assignment form) **16**		
☐ (3) Monitors newsroom scanners for local emergencies such as fire and police (emergency services call log form) **16**		
☐ (4) Plans news coverage **16**		
☐ (5) Maintains news beat/future files (news beat/future file form) **16**		
☐ (6) Attends newscast planning conference **21**		
☐ (7) Is responsible for hard/soft news stories in the newscast **23**		
☐ (8) Creates hard news newscast format segment (newscast format form) **23**		
☐ (9) Assigns videographers; keeps videographer assignment board updated (remote assignment form) **23**		

PREPRODUCTION

☐ (10) Assigns video editors; keeps video editor assignment board updated (editor/editing reservation form) 23
☐ (11) Continues to monitor scanners, news sources, phone calls to update and add to the format 25

NEWS PRODUCER (NP)

☐ (1) Reports to the executive producer 16
☐ (2) Works with the assignment editor 18
☐ (3) Attends newscast planning conference 21
☐ (4) Coordinates news stories for each newscast 26
☐ (5) Assigns graphic needs (graphic design request form) 26
☐ (6) Monitors/reviews all video for the newscast 26
☐ (7) Coordinates videotape into the newscast 29
☐ (8) Helps plan soft news/feature/series packages 29
☐ (9) Monitors feature packages (video production calendar form) 29
☐ (10) Keeps newscast program format board updated 29
☐ (11) Writes lead-in for feature packages 30
☐ (12) Times the newscast from the updated format board 30
☐ (13) Creates/copies/distributes the format/rundown sheet (format/rundown sheet form) 30
☐ (14) Creates character generator copy master list (character generator copy/credits form) 31
☐ (15) Turns over to telecine operator/videotape recorder operator videotape masters/film sources (video sources form) 31

TALENT (T)

☐ (1) Auditions for/is chosen by the news director (talent audition form) 18
☐ (2) Attends newscast planning conference 21
☐ (3) Accepts news reporting/feature producing assignments 22

EDITORIALIST (E)

☐ (1) Auditions for/is chosen by news director 19
☐ (2) Attends newscast planning conference 21
☐ (3) Researches assigned editorial 23
☐ (4) Writes editorial 28
☐ (5) Submits editorial to the news director for approval 28
☐ (6) Answers mail responses to editorials 28

PRODUCTION

NEWS PRODUCER (NP)

☐ (1) Makes a last minute check with the studio director and talent 39
☐ (2) Monitors the newscast from the control room during the production 39
☐ (3) Communicates with the studio director on newscast content/format problems changes during the production 39
☐ (4) Makes content decisions with final timing of the newscast 49

TALENT (T)

☐ (1) Reviews format/rundown sheet for newscast order/changes/updates 41
☐ (2) Secures talent copy(ies) of the newscast script 41
☐ (3) Reads script for familiarity/pronunciation problems 43
☐ (4) Marks teleprompter script copy for reading interpretation 43
☐ (5) Gets dressed for the newscast; applies make-up 44
☐ (6) Reports to the studio set; maintains spike marks 44
☐ (7) Performs microphone checks at the audio director's request 44
☐ (8) Checks teleprompter monitors for reading ease and light reflection 44
☐ (9) Has floor director check make-up and make repairs 44
☐ (10) Alerts floor director when ready 44
☐ (11) Stands by with floor director's call 47
☐ (12) Begins with floor director's signal from studio director/camera tally light 47
☐ (13) Follows floor director's communications 49
☐ (14) Repairs make-up during commercial breaks 49
☐ (15) Holds studio position; prepares for postproduction; cleans up anchor desk with studio director's wrap call 50

EDITORIALIST (E)

☐ (1) Reviews format/rundown sheet for newscast order/changes/updates 41
☐ (2) Secures editorialist copy of script 41
☐ (3) Reads script for familiarity/pronunciation problems 43
☐ (4) Marks teleprompter script copy for reading interpretation 43
☐ (5) Gets dressed for the newscast; applies make-up 44
☐ (6) Reports to the studio set 44
☐ (7) Checks teleprompter monitors for reading ease 44

POSTPRODUCTION

NEWS PRODUCER (NP)

(If the newscast just produced is a tape-delayed telecast, some postproduction may be undertaken. If so, the news producer may be involved.)

☐ (1) Assumes the decision-making role to add or redo elements of the newscast 51
☐ (2) Communicates those elements of the producing or production stages of the newscast that will become a part of the postproduction process 51
☐ (3) Continues as in the production stage 51

TALENT (T)

(If the newscast just produced is a tape-delayed telecast, some postproduction may be undertaken. If so, the studio talent may be involved.)

☐ (1) Readies for those elements of the production that involve the talent in postproduction 52
☐ (2) Continues as in the production stage 52

EDITORIALIST (E)

(If the newscast just produced is a tape-delayed telecast, some postproduction may be undertaken. If so, the editorialist may be involved.)

☐ (1) Prepares for those elements of the production that involve the editorialist in postproduction 52
☐ (2) Continues as in the production stage 52

(8) Has floor director check make-up and make repairs **44**
(9) Alerts floor director when ready **45**
(10) Stands by with floor director's call **49**
(11) Begins with floor director's signal from studio director/ camera tally light **49**
(12) Follows floor director's instructions **49**

REPORTERS/WRITERS (R/W)

(1) Are hired/chosen by the executive producer **19**
(2) Are assigned/maintain a news beat **20**
(3) Attend newscast planning conference **21**
(4) Receive news assignment from assignment editor **21**
(5) Research news assignment, follow leads, make phone calls **21**
(6) Arrange video shoot **21**
(7) Contact assigned videographer **23**
(8) Contact assigned video editor **23**
(9) Secure source videotape stock for location shoot **26**
(10) Produce video shoot, interview, collect information **27**
(11) Keep remote video log (remote log form) **27**
(12) Assist videographer on location **27**
(13) Return to newsroom, write story **27**
(14) Indicate/confirm graphic needs **29**
(15) Submit script to the script editor **29**
(16) Type edited news story for the teleprompter **30**
(17) Do the voice-over recording from edited script copy **30**
(18) Edit/oversee videotape editing with video editor **30**
(19) Complete edited master clipsheet (edited master clipsheet form) **30**
(20) Submit master videotape and clipsheet to the news producer **30**

FEATURE PRODUCER (FP)

(1) Is hired/chosen by the news director **20**
(2) Attends newscast planning conference **21**
(3) Receives feature package assignment from the news producer or proposes feature package/treatment to the news producer (package treatment form) **21**
(4) Researches feature content, follows leads **21**
(5) Makes phone calls, interviews news maker and/or prospective talent **21**
(6) Writes treatment for feature package (package treatment form) **21**
(7) Submits treatment/proposal for approval to the executive producer or the news director **22**
(8) Performs preproduction tasks: prepares script, script breakdown, and shot list; scouts location (television script form, video script/storyboard form, script breakdown form, remote camera shot list forms, location site survey form) **22**
(9) Sets a production schedule/appointment(s) with news maker/talent, arranges location shoot (production schedule form) **23**
(10) Contacts assigned videographer; makes travel arrangements **23**
(11) Contacts and sets editing time with assigned videotape editor (editor/editing reservation form) **24**
(12) Produces/directs location videotaping; interviews talent (talent release form) **26**
(13) Keeps remote video log (remote log form) **27**
(14) Assists the videographer on location **27**
(15) Returns to the station with the videographer **27**

POSTPRODUCTION

PRODUCTION

PREPRODUCTION

- [ ] (16) Writes production script; secures copyright clearances (television script form, video script/storyboard form) **28**
- [ ] (17) Submits graphic design request form to graphic artist/producer (graphic design form) **28**
- [ ] (18) Prepares editing work sheet (editing work sheet form) **28**
- [ ] (19) Prepares editing cue sheet (editing cue sheet form) **28**
- [ ] (20) Oversees videotape editing with videotape editor **28**
- [ ] (21) Completes edited master clipsheet for news producer (edited master clipsheet form) **28**
- [ ] (22) Turns videotape master over to the news producer **28**

GRAPHIC ARTIST/PRODUCER (G)

- [ ] (1) Receives graphic design request form from the news producer/reporter/writer/feature producer **26**
- [ ] (2) Lists assigned stories; determines graphics needs **26**
- [ ] (3) Prepares/creates graphics **26**
- [ ] (4) Reports completed graphics summary list to the news producer (graphics summary rundown form) **30**
- [ ] (5) Distributes graphics sources/list to the assistant director, technical director, telecine operator, and videotape operator (video sources form) **30**

SCRIPT EDITOR (SE)

- [ ] (1) Is hired/chosen by the executive producer **29**
- [ ] (2) Reads/edits all script copy before the final script is typed **30**
- [ ] (3) Monitors newscast script from final draft to teleprompter **30**
- [ ] (4) Reviews newscast format board and format/rundown sheet **31**
- [ ] (5) Types remaining newscast script copy for the teleprompter **31**
- [ ] (6) Prints/provides copies of the final newscast production script **31**
- [ ] (7) Distributes the script to the talent, teleprompter operator, studio director, and news producer **31**

VIDEOGRAPHER(S) (VG)

- [ ] (1) Assigned by assignment editor to producer or reporter/writer **23**
- [ ] (2) Meets with the producer or reporter/writer **24**
- [ ] (3) Reserves remote video recording equipment and news vehicle **25**
- [ ] (4) Picks up remote video recording equipment and signs out news vehicle (equipment checklist form) **26**
- [ ] (5) Assists feature producer or reporter/writer on location **26**
- [ ] (6) Sets up video camera, videotape recorder, lighting instruments, and microphones on location **26**
- [ ] (7) Videotapes according to the directions of the reporter/writer or producer **27**
- [ ] (8) Removes record button from the videocassette; labels the videotape cassette **27**
- [ ] (9) Strikes location set-up **27**
- [ ] (10) Returns with the producer or reporter/writer to the newsroom **27**
- [ ] (11) Reports arrival to the assignment editor (remote assignment form) **27**
- [ ] (12) Returns remote video recording equipment and reports any damage, malfunctioning, or maintenance needs **28**

VIDEO EDITOR(S) (VE)

- (1) Assigned by assignment editor to the producer or reporter/writer **23**
- (2) Meets with the producer or reporter/writer **24**
- (3) Evaluates editing needs; requests special hardware **24**
- (4) Reserves video editing suite; maintains reservation board (editor/editing reservation form) **24**
- (5) Reviews editing cue sheet with the producer or reporter/writer **30**
- (6) Edits with the reporter/writer or producer **30**
- (7) Defers final editing decisions to the producer or reporter/writer **30**
- (8) Corrects video levels; mixes audio tracks **30**
- (9) Removes record button; labels videocassette and case **30**

STUDIO DIRECTOR (D)

- (1) Attends newscast planning conference **22**
- (2) Supervises studio production crew **31**
- (3) Approves news set audio and lighting plots **31**
- (4) Secures a copy of the format/rundown sheet from the news producer and the script from the script editor **31**
- (5) Reviews/studies the format/rundown sheet **31**
- (6) Works on/prepares the script **31**
- (7) Creates the camera blocking plot and camera shot list (studio camera blocking plot form, studio camera shot list form) **31**
- (8) Schedules crew call, holds production meeting with studio crew when necessary **31**
- (9) Meets with the assistant director **32**

- (1) Monitors all studio/control room/master control set-ups/readiness **39**
- (2) Orients to assigned video source monitors **41**
- (3) Checks intercom network connections and response stations **41**
- (4) Awaits "ready" cue from production personnel: audio director, camera operators, lighting director, production assistant, technical director, floor director, talent, video engineer, videotape recorder operator **46**
- (5) Calls stand-by cue to studio/control room/master control personnel **47**
- (6) Calls a "ready to roll tape" to the videotape recorder operator; calls the cue to roll videotape **47**
- (7) Awaits real clock time or begins when ready; counts down to the newscast opening **47**
- (8) Directs the script with preproduction notations and cues; readies/takes video/audio sources noted in the script **48**
- (9) Confers with the news producer for content/format decisions **49**
- (10) Closes newscast; announces postproduction **49**
- (11) Announces the postproduction needs **49**
- (12) Calls for a studio wrap **50**

(If the newscast just produced is a tape-delayed telecast, some postproduction may be undertaken. If so, the studio director may be involved.)

- (1) Assumes responsibility and decision-making role to add or redo elements of the newscast that involve studio production errors or problems; communicates with the news producer/news director **51**
- (2) Alerts specific crew who will be involved in postproduction **51**
- (3) Continues as in the production stage **51**

ASSISTANT DIRECTOR (AD)

- (1) Appointed by the studio director **32**
- (2) Reviews/studies the format/rundown sheet **32**
- (3) Meets with the studio director **32**
- (4) Attends crew call for each newscast; attends production meeting when scheduled **36**

- (1) Assists the studio director with production details **39**
- (2) Checks format/rundown sheet for changes/updates **39**
- (3) Orients to all video source monitors **41**
- (4) Checks intercom network connections **41**
- (5) Reviews character generator master list/recorded copy with production assistant **42**
- (6) Resets countdown timer(s), checks stop watch(es)/counters for front, back, and segment times during newscast **45**
- (7) Prepares to follow script for the studio director **47**
- (8) Reads loudly clock/timer countdowns to opening/other cues during the production **47**
- (9) Reads expected out-cues to all video stories/packages **48**
- (10) Keeps close tabs on all timed prerecorded video sources **48**
- (11) Operates/advances the telecine on remote or communicates cues to telecine operator to advance manually **48**
- (12) Operates remote video playback on cue **48**

(If the newscast just produced is a tape-delayed telecast, some postproduction may be undertaken. If so, the assistant director may be involved.)

- (1) Readies those crew members who may be involved in postproduction work on the newscast **51**
- (2) Continues as in the production stage **51**

	PREPRODUCTION	PRODUCTION	POSTPRODUCTION
TECHNICAL DIRECTOR (TD)	(1) Reviews/studies the format/rundown sheet 32 (2) Checks with the videotape recorder operator/video engineer 32 (3) Updates the video sources checklist (video sources form) 32 (4) Checks videotape playback/record monitors 32 (5) Attends crew call for each newscast; attends production meeting when scheduled 36	(1) Familiarizes self with the format/rundown sheet and any changes updates 39 (2) Checks intercom network connections 42 (3) Checks video playback routing through the switcher 45 (4) Checks video levels of videotape playback sources with videotape recorder operator 46 (5) Sets video clip levels for mattes on switcher 46 (6) Presets mix effects buses for special effects 46 (7) Checks/presets any other special effects equipment available 46 (8) Alerts studio director when ready 47 (9) Listens to/readies/responds to studio director's commands 48 (10) Switches appropriate video sources 48 (11) Prepares for postproduction needs; stops down the switcher at the studio director's wrap call 50 (13) Readies all character generator screen copy 48 (14) Prepares for postproduction needs from crew; helps complete studio wrap 49	(If the newscast just produced is a tape-delayed telecast, some postproduction may be undertaken. If so, the technical director may be involved.) (1) Prepares to add or redo those elements of the newscast in postproduction that involve the switcher 51 (2) Communicates to the video recorder operator what video sources will be involved in postproduction 51 (3) Continues as in the production stage 51
PRODUCTION ASSISTANT (PA)	(1) Reviews/studies the format/rundown sheet 32 (2) Receives character generator master list from the news producer 32 (3) Begins entering character generator copy for the newscast 32 (4) Attends crew call for each newscast; attends production meeting when scheduled 37	(1) Enters last minute data changes into the character generator 39 (2) Reviews recorded character generator information with the assistant director 42 (3) Keeps the character generator screen information current 42 (4) Alerts the studio director when ready 47 (5) Advances character generator copy when the technical director clears the matte from the program line 48 (6) Alerts the studio director/assistant director to unused character generator copy 48 (7) Prepares for postproduction needs; turns off the character generator at the studio director's wrap call 50	(If the newscast just produced is a tape-delayed telecast, some postproduction may be undertaken. If so, the production assistant may be involved.) (1) Prepares to ready those elements of the production that involve the character generator for postproduction 51 (2) Continues as in the production stage 51
AUDIO DIRECTOR (A)	(1) Reviews/studies the format/rundown sheet 32 (2) Creates/submits the news set audio plot to the studio director for approval (news set audio plot) 33 (3) Begins setting out microphones to be used for the newscast 33 (4) Secures prerecorded audio recordings; makes cartridge transfers 33 (5) Checks all sound recorded sources; cues sources up 33 (6) Attends crew call for each newscast; attends production meeting when scheduled 37	(1) Reviews the format/rundown sheet for studio microphone needs, prerecorded audio sources, and playback audio needs; updates playback audio needs 40 (2) Checks studio microphone connections 42 (3) Checks intercom network connections 42 (4) Sets levels for playback audio cartridge sources 44 (5) Checks/re-cues all prerecorded audio sources 44 (6) Patches/checks audio foldback sound to the studio 44 (7) Calls for studio talent microphone checks; sets levels for each microphone 44 (8) Sets levels for playback video sources 46 (9) Alerts studio director when ready 47 (10) Awaits studio director's opening cues 47 (11) Follows studio director's calls during the newscast 48 (12) Prepares for postproduction needs; strikes the audio set-up at the studio director's call for a wrap 50	(If the newscast just produced is a tape-delayed telecast, some postproduction may be undertaken. If so, the audio director may be involved.) (1) Prepares to ready those elements of the production that involve audio sources for postproduction 51 (2) Continues as in the production stage 51
FLOOR DIRECTOR (F)	(1) Reviews/studies the format/rundown sheet 33 (2) Begins studio news set set-up; organizes the set 34 (3) Attends crew call for each newscast; attends production meeting when scheduled 37	(1) Reviews the format/rundown sheet for studio expectations, order of newscast, and updates 40 (2) Organizes the studio set for readiness; replaces props on spike marks 42	(If the newscast just produced is a tape-delayed telecast, some postproduction may be undertaken. If so, the floor director may be involved.) (1) Prepares to ready those elements of the production

that involve the studio and studio personnel for postproduction **52**

☐ (2) Continues as in the production stage **52**

(3) Checks on talent; monitors their readiness **45**
(4) Checks intercom network connections **45**
(5) Checks on camera operators; monitors their readiness **45**
(6) Checks on lighting/instruments/pattern working order **46**
(7) Checks audio foldback sound in the studio **46**
(8) Makes make-up check on talent; repairs powdering **46**
(9) Alerts studio director when the studio is ready **47**
(10) Communicates the studio director's commands to studio personnel **47**
(11) Calls/maintains readiness in the studio **47**
(12) Repeats all countdowns to the studio down to the 2-second call **47**
(13) Signals camera(s) "on" to talent **47**
(14) Maintains communication between the studio director and the studio **48**
(15) Communicates during commercial breaks to the talent any changes from the studio director or news producer **48**
(16) Repairs talent make-up during breaks **48**
(17) Communicates to the studio director any information from the studio **49**
(18) Relays the studio director's calls for hold positions/postproduction/wrap **50**

STUDIO CAMERA OPERATORS (CO)

(1) Review/study the format/rundown sheet **34**
(2) Receive camera shot list from the studio director **34**
(3) Check cameras for operation **34**
(4) Choose lens filter **34**
(5) Balance pedestal **34**
(6) Adjust camera handles **34**
(7) Set pan/tilt friction **34**
(8) Select external video option for the camera monitor **35**
(9) Attend crew call for each newscast; attend production meeting when scheduled **37**

(1) Review format/rundown sheets for studio camera needs/changes/updates **40**
(2) Check camera for zoom, pan, tilt, dolly, truck, pedestal, and arc control **42**
(3) Secure adequate cable behind camera for movement flexibility **42**
(4) Check intercom network connection **42**
(5) Practice required shots of the talent **42**
(6) Check lens filter choice **42**
(7) Maintain depth of field focus during/after changes in position **43**
(8) Set opening shots; alert the studio director when ready **46**
(9) Maintain ready position until new set-up is called **48**
(10) Listen/follow the studio director's calls during newscast production **49**
(11) Hold studio positions; prepare for postproduction; strike camera with the studio director's wrap call **50**

(If the newscast just produced is a tape-delayed telecast, some postproduction may be undertaken. If so, the studio cameras may be involved.)

☐ (1) Prepare to ready those elements of the production that involve the studio cameras for postproduction **52**
☐ (2) Continue as in the production stage **52**

TELEPROMPTER OPERATOR (TO)

(1) Reviews the format/rundown sheet for production order **34**
(2) Sets up teleprompter bed **34**
(3) Secures teleprompter script copy from the script editor **34**
(4) Prepares to run script copy for camera monitor **34**
(5) Attends crew call for each newscast; attends production meeting when scheduled **37**

(1) Reviews the format/rundown sheet for order of newscast and any changes/updates **41**
(2) Secures teleprompter script copy for the teleprompter **42**
(3) Prepares script copy for the teleprompter bed **43**
(4) Checks video reproduction of the script at camera monitors **43**
(5) Permits talent to check reading pleasure and practice with script; checks foldback sound in studio **44**
(6) Alerts the floor director when ready **45**
(7) Awaits the floor director's cue to begin **47**
(8) Follows talent carefully; keeps script copy at the desired screen height **48**
(9) Holds studio position; prepares for postproduction; strikes the teleprompter at the studio director's wrap call **50**

(If the newscast just produced is a tape-delayed telecast, some postproduction may be undertaken. If so, the teleprompter may be involved.)

☐ (1) Prepares to ready those elements of the production that involve the teleprompter in postproduction **52**
☐ (2) Continues as in the production stage **52**

TELECINE OPERATOR (TC)

PREPRODUCTION
- [ ] (1) Reviews/studies the format/rundown sheet **35**
- [ ] (2) Secures film sources from the news producer and/or graphic artist/producer **35**
- [ ] (3) Attends crew call for each newscast; attends production meeting when scheduled **37**

PRODUCTION
- [ ] (1) Reviews/studies the format/rundown sheet and graphic design list for newscast order and any changes/updates **41**
- [ ] (2) Loads the telecine with slides/film, as necessary **42**
- [ ] (3) Checks the telecine operation and order of film sources **46**
- [ ] (4) Checks the intercom network connections **46**
- [ ] (5) Communicates to the assistant director when ready **47**
- [ ] (6) Operates/advances the telecine during the newscast or monitors remote control by the assistant director in the control room **48**
- [ ] (7) Stands by for changes/corrections during the newscast; reloads sources **49**
- [ ] (8) Holds telecine operation; prepares for postproduction; strikes film sources with the studio director's call for a wrap **50**

POSTPRODUCTION
(If the newscast just produced is a tape-delayed telecast, some postproduction may be undertaken. If so, the technical director may be involved.)
- [ ] (1) Prepares to ready those elements of the production that involve the telecine in postproduction **52**
- [ ] (2) Continues as in the production stage **52**

LIGHTING DIRECTOR (LD)

PREPRODUCTION
- [ ] (1) Designs, submits for approval, and checks news set lighting plot (news set lighting plot form) **35**
- [ ] (2) Adjusts/aims lights and makes adjustments for hair and clothing **35**
- [ ] (3) Attends crew call for each newscast; attends production meeting when scheduled **37**

PRODUCTION
- [ ] (1) Reviews the format/rundown sheet for newscast order and any changes in lighting needs or updates **39**
- [ ] (2) Checks lighting pattern on studio set/light instruments **39**
- [ ] (3) Checks lighting effects over studio camera monitors **40**
- [ ] (4) Checks unwanted light reflection off teleprompter monitors **40**
- [ ] (5) Makes lighting intensity/light instrument changes **40**
- [ ] (6) Alerts the studio director when lighting is ready **40**
- [ ] (7) Listens for the studio director's call for lighting cues/changes **47**
- [ ] (8) Prepares for postproduction; strikes lighting with studio director's call for a studio wrap **50**

POSTPRODUCTION
(If the newscast just produced is a tape-delayed telecast, some postproduction may be undertaken. If so, the lighting director may be involved.)
- [ ] (1) Readies those lighting elements of the production that involve the lighting director in postproduction **52**
- [ ] (2) Continues as in the production stage **52**

VIDEOTAPE RECORDER OPERATOR (VTRO)

PREPRODUCTION
- [ ] (1) Checks operation of video recorder(s)/playback units **35**
- [ ] (2) Performs preventive maintenance **35**
- [ ] (3) Checks the format/rundown sheet for video source playback requirements/order **35**
- [ ] (4) Secures master videotapes for A-roll and B-roll from the news producer **35**
- [ ] (5) Prepares/performs A-roll and B-roll videotape dubbing **35**
- [ ] (6) Chooses videotape playback and record videotape decks; informs technical director of choices **35**

PRODUCTION
- [ ] (1) Reviews the format/rundown sheet for videotape playback/recording needs/changes/updates **41**
- [ ] (2) Chooses playback/record videotape recorders; informs technical director of choices **45**
- [ ] (3) Sets video levels of videotape sources with the technical director **46**
- [ ] (4) Cues up playback machines for B-roll videotape **46**
- [ ] (5) Threads record machine for dub of the newscast **46**
- [ ] (6) Switches remote control of playback videotape recorders to the assistant director in the control room **46**
- [ ] (7) Alerts the studio director when ready **46**
- [ ] (8) Responds to the studio director's call for "ready to roll tape"/"roll tape" **47**
- [ ] (9) Monitors playback/record videotape machines **49**
- [ ] (10) Prepares for postproduction needs; strikes videotape recording with the studio director's call for a wrap **50**
- [ ] (11) Rewinds videotapes; labels videotapes and videotape storage cases **50**

POSTPRODUCTION
(If the newscast just produced is a tape-delayed telecast, some postproduction may be undertaken. If so, the videotape recorder operator may be involved.)
- [ ] (1) Readies those video recording elements of the production that involve the videotape recorder operator in postproduction **52**
- [ ] (2) Continues as in the production stage **52**

VIDEO ENGINEER (VEG)

PREPRODUCTION
- [ ] (1) Checks cameras with camera operators **35**
- [ ] (2) Does preventive maintenance **35**
- [ ] (3) Uncaps camera lenses **36**
- [ ] (4) Checks teleprompter monitors on cameras **36**
- [ ] (5) Sets video levels/lenses with studio lights **36**
- [ ] (6) Routes external signal to camera monitors for camera operator use **36**
- [ ] (7) Checks tally light operation of cameras **36**

PRODUCTION
- [ ] (1) Readies studio cameras for videotaping/shading **40**
- [ ] (2) Checks video levels of cameras with lighting on the set **40**
- [ ] (3) Alerts studio director when ready **40**
- [ ] (4) Monitors video level of cameras during the newscast **49**
- [ ] (5) Alerts the studio director to soft focused cameras during the newscast **49**
- [ ] (6) Prepares for postproduction needs; caps cameras with the studio director's call for a wrap **50**

POSTPRODUCTION
(If the newscast just produced is a tape-delayed telecast, some postproduction may be undertaken. If so, the video engineer may be involved.)
- [ ] (1) Readies those video production elements of the newscast that involve video engineering in postproduction **52**
- [ ] (2) Continues as in the production stage **52**

Chapter 2

Processes of Television Newscast Production

THE PREPRODUCTION PROCESS

One of the most detailed and demanding preproduction processes in all of television production is the process of producing television news. The extent of news preproduction importance and structure is characterized by the existence of professional organizations, such as the Radio-Television News Directors Association (RTNDA), dedicated almost exclusively to the preproduction stages of news only.

The process of newscast producing is a series of highly structured and defined stages of television production unlike that of most other television genres. Equally unlike other studio production genres, the preproduction process of the television newscast permits very little creative initiative.

• Personnel

Deciding what is an ideal or normal number of preproduction newscast staff is difficult. In commercial newscast production, the size of the preproduction staff is a function of the size of the available budget; however, in academia there is generally little difficulty in creating a preproduction staff of almost any size. As in most other television genres, the size of a commercial broadcast market or the size of a television news production class will have as much to do with the number of newscast producers and preproduction staff as with the budget, the size of the production facility, and the amount of production hardware available.

A 1989 Radio-Television News Directors Association pamphlet on careers in radio and television news included seven producing roles (involving a staff of 22) for a medium broadcast market.[1] The seven roles include a news director, an executive producer or assistant news director, an assignment editor, an anchor/reporter, a reporter, a videographer/video editor, and a news producer. The personnel roles included in this worktext build on this list, but expand preproduction roles.

But for a few exceptional cases (e.g., talent and direct assistants), whether personnel are hired (as in commercial news production) or chosen for roles (as in academia) is not always indicated. Those roles so designated as "hired or chosen" require a strong superior/subordinate relationship and are thus indicated.

Finally, preproduction personnel in television news production must also take into account the studio production crew. The studio crew has to perform what is clearly defined as preproduction tasks and will be included with preproduction personnel.

News director (ND) In television newscast producing, the role title for the supervising officer of the news operation is different from the equivalent role title in other television production genres. The news director has the top role in the production of television news. In a commercial television station, the news director is directly responsible to the general manager. The news director controls newsroom personnel, the newscast budget, news philosophy, policy and judgment, and the telecast news product itself, the newscast, for which the news director is ultimately responsible.

Executive news producer (EP) Second in command and responsibility in television newscast producing is the

[1] Vernon A. Stone, *Careers in Radio and Television News* (Washington, D.C.: Radio-Television News Directors Association, 1989).

FIGURE 2–1
Newscast development. Designing and developing a newscast begins with newscast design and format ideas, budgeting, set design, audio and lighting plots, and the audition and hiring of talent.

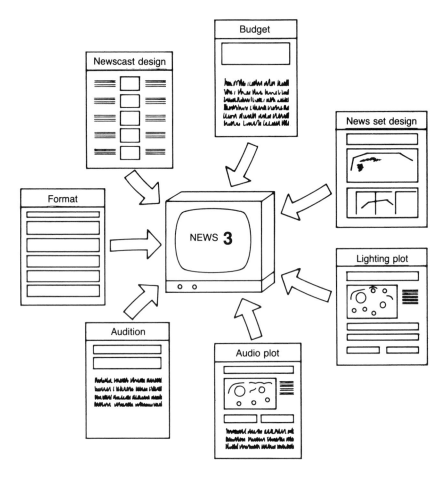

executive news producer or, as the role is titled in some news operations, the assistant news director. As the news director controls and is responsible for the whole newscast, the executive producer controls and is responsible for the day-to-day operation of each newscast. This places the executive producer in charge of managing the newsroom, the newscast-by-newscast format, and supervising news producers.

Assignment editor (AE)   The basic news producing work begins with the assignment editor. Directly responsible to the executive producer, the assignment editor is the journalist of the newsroom. The assignment editor keeps abreast of breaking news; news sources; news coverage; future news; and the assignment of news gathering to reporter/writers, feature producers, videographers, and video editors. The news content choices for each newscast are the primary responsibility of the assignment editor.

News producer (NP)   The news producer does the work assigned (news stories and feature packages) by the assignment editor. The news producer monitors, coordinates, approves, and updates the work of reporter/writers, feature producers, videographers, and video editors. The news producer is one of the final hands on any individual newscast, writing lead-ins, finalizing the format, timing the newscast, overseeing the character generator master copy, and approving the video sources into the newscast. The news producer plans feature packages and series for future newscasts.

Reporters/writers (R/W)   Some of the most important people in a newsroom are the reporters/writers. Taking information, making news judgments, writing and rewriting news copy to be understood by the television audience in a single hearing, and videotaping or choosing video images to tell a story require the skills that define and distinguish television news from any other news medium. The reporters/writers are responsible to the assignment editor for their news story assignments and to the news producer for accomplishing the journalism skills necessary to take the stories assigned to production and telecast.

Editorialist (E)   A decision made early in any newscast planning is the topic for an editorial. As a daily newspaper without an editorial page, so too, increasingly, is a television newscast without an editorial. An editorialist becomes a very important spokesperson for the news organization. The editorialist is directly responsible to the news director. The topic for an editorial is assigned at the newscast planning conference (or at a separate editorial board meeting) for every newscast.

Graphic artist/producer (G)   With the development of sophisticated and creative graphics production hardware and software in the 1980s, there are very few news operations without some creative form of video screen graphics production capability. Admittedly, the production of graphics with 35mm mounted slides is still common. In some operations, while 35mm slides may not

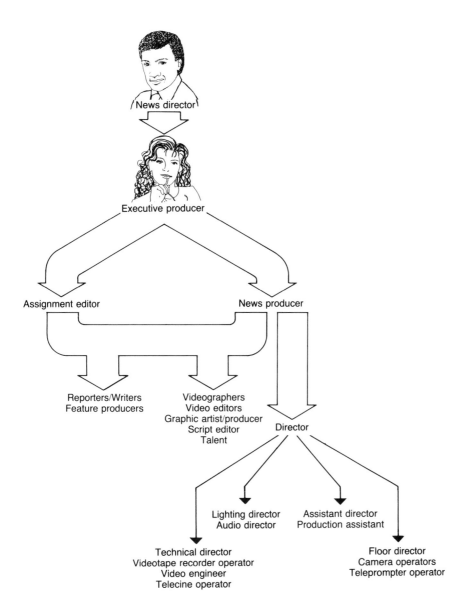

FIGURE 2–2
News organization personnel. This organizational chart places most producing and production roles in their respective supervisory and subordinate positions.

be produced on the premises, the same 35mm graphics are purchased for imaging news stories. The graphics may be computer designed and produced, created and photographed as part of the newsroom producing process, or chosen from a 35mm slide storage unit. The graphics producer is responsible for creating and/or assembling the graphics requested by the assignment editor, the reporter/writer, or the feature producer.

Script editor (SE) The larger the newscast producing operation and the longer the television newscast (one hour versus one-half hour) the greater the need for one person to be directly responsible for the script for the program. The script editor in some news operations edits, types, and makes copies of the script for the studio teleprompter production and personnel needing a copy of the script. The script editor's role includes monitoring the process of script production from the newsroom to the studio.

Feature producer (FP) The feature producer, often selected from among the staff reporters/writers, is assigned

to plan the production of either a longer video package (usually of soft news quality) or a series of packages on one theme (as is common during ratings sweep periods). The feature producer can initiate the package or be assigned to the package by the assignment editor or the news producer. The feature producer is responsible for the longer preproduction process involved in the production of video packages. In some news operations the feature producer will also be assigned a videographer and a video editor.

Videographer (VG) A videographer is a video camera photographer. The videographer has the skills of remote videotaping with video camera, videotape recorder, location lighting, and sound recording. The assignment editor assigns the videographer to a reporter/writer or feature producer. The videographer is responsible for videotaping hard or soft news events under the direction of the reporter/writer or feature producer. The videographer is also responsible for reserving the necessary videotaping equipment for the day and time required by the reporter/writer or feature producer.

Video editor (VE) The video editor is a person with videotape postproduction editing skills. In many news operations, reporters/writers, feature producers, and videographers may double as their own video editors. When a reporter or feature producer does not do the editing, a video editor will be assigned to the reporter/writer or feature producer. The video editor is responsible for reserving an editing suite for the day and time required for editing the videotape under the direction of the reporter/writer or feature producer.

Talent (T) The talent for television news usually includes anchor(s), co-anchor, weathercaster, and sportscaster. All talent roles generally imply some reporting and feature producing. In many news operations, anchors are required and often want to get involved in reporting and producing the news. Anchors may also involve themselves in editing the news copy of the reporter/writer to make it their own in style and familiarity. Weathercasters and sportscasters have their specialized news areas.

Studio director (D) The studio director is in charge of the studio production of the newscast and the studio production crew. The studio director communicates with the entire production crew, principally through a crew call or production meeting sometime before newscast taping or airing. The studio director prepares a camera placement and blocking plot and a camera shot list during preproduction. The studio director's primary preproduction responsibility is to secure and prepare the newscast script for directing. The studio director needs time to prepare the script with directorial notation cues. The studio director has to be familiar with the format/rundown sheet as well as with the newscast script.

Assistant director (AD) The assistant director's preproduction responsibility focuses on becoming familiar with the format/rundown sheet. Apart from that, the assistant director is in the service of the news director.

Technical director (TD) The technical director best prepares for switching the newscast by working with and becoming familiar with the format/rundown sheet. Equally important in preproduction is knowledge of the video sources assigned by the video recording operator to the control room and the production switcher. These video playback videotape machines and control room monitor assignments are reported on the video sources form from the videotape recorder operator.

Production assistant (PA) Some of the production assistant's task responsibilities are accomplished in preproduction. Entering and recording all character generator copy that will be used is the primary responsibility of the production assistant in preproduction.

Audio director (A) The audio director has a number of preproduction responsibilities. The primary preproduction task is preparing the news set audio plot. This has to be created and submitted to the studio director for approval. Hardware for studio production has to be set out, any sound recording not wedded to videotape or film will have to be dubbed to cartridges and cued up, and any prerecorded audio sources have to be checked and gain levels set. The audio director has to be familiar with the format/rundown sheet for the newscast.

Floor director (F) The floor director's preproduction responsibilities entail familiarity with the format/rundown sheet and the set-up and organization of the studio news set for production.

Teleprompter operator (TO) The teleprompter operator's responsibility in preproduction involves preparing the script copy for the talent via camera monitors. The prompter operator must be familiar with the format/rundown sheet.

Studio camera operators (CO) The studio camera operators are responsible for preparing the cameras for production and reviewing their assigned camera shots. Preproduction tasks involve choosing filters (e.g., star filters if studio lights are part of news set shots), selecting external video (for viewing the control room line video during production), balancing the pedestal of the cameras, and setting friction pads for camera pan and tilt. Familiarity with the format/rundown sheet assists camera operators in knowing what is expected of them during production.

Telecine operator (TC) The telecine may be involved if the production is using 16mm or 35mm film sources. The telecine operator needs to know what film sources are needed during the newscast. When 35mm slides are used, the order of entry into the telecine and proper positioning can involve a lot of time and accuracy. The telecine operator will need the graphics summary rundown form from the graphics producer.

Lighting director (LD) Most of the lighting director's role responsibility lies in preproduction: lighting the studio news set. This task requires creating a news set lighting plot and submitting it to the studio director for approval. Besides the role of lighting design, the lighting director must regularly check the lighting instruments for both bulb loss and instrument direction and focus. The lighting director needs to be sensitive in preproduction to reflection and glare in the eyes of the talent from prompter monitors.

Videotape recorder operator (VTRO) The videotape recorder operator has the preproduction responsibility to ready all playback videotape decks for alternating playback video sources. Should the newscast require videotape recording, assigning a videotape record deck will also be necessary. Control room video and audio signals will have to be routed and checked. The technical director must be informed of the playback videotape deck assignments so the switcher can be assigned to feed signals from those decks through the switcher.

Video engineer (VE) The video engineer is responsible for the proper maintenance of the studio cameras and teleprompter monitors on the front of the cameras. Uncapping cameras, routing the external signal to the cameras, checking tally light operation, and setting camera lenses to studio set light levels completes the video engineer's preproduction tasks.

• Preproduction Stages

Television newscasts require a large preproduction staff with a lot of timely personnel interaction and producing task interface. Many elements must come together before the newscast goes to the studio. When the program is telecast live, as are most television newscasts, the pressure to interact and interface is more demanding.

Hiring and/or choosing newscast producing or production personnel (ND 1)   The news director generally handles the hiring and/or choosing of all production personnel. In some television facilities, the studio crew may already be a part of the station's full-time personnel and will serve the newscast as it would any other studio production of the station.

Keeping the budget and authorizing expenses (ND 2)   The news director has complete control of the television newscast and the budget for the program. The budget usually includes above- and below-the-line salaries as well as the cost of all news services coming into the newsroom, studio production, videotape recording and

editing hardware, production of graphics, computerized newsroom, and generally all expenses associated with the newsroom facility, including supplies and newscast and talent promotions. All expenses require the authorization of the news director before purchase. (See the production budget form.)

Designing and/or deciding the studio news set (ND 3)   A news director has creative control over the design and construction of the studio news set. While the news director may be qualified to design a set, many news directors will seek professional creative help in the design and construction of a set. Consultants and design artists are available for news set design through trade magazines. (See the news set design form.)

Designing and deciding newscast production values (ND 4)   A news director also has control over all newscast production values, which includes the design of all video and audio elements in the production of the newscast from opening titling, music, and announcer copy to the degree of framing of talent, the content of bumpers, and the extent of credits per newscast. Newscast production values are designed on storyboard units. The storyboard facilitates the communication of designed production values to studio and control room crew responsible for

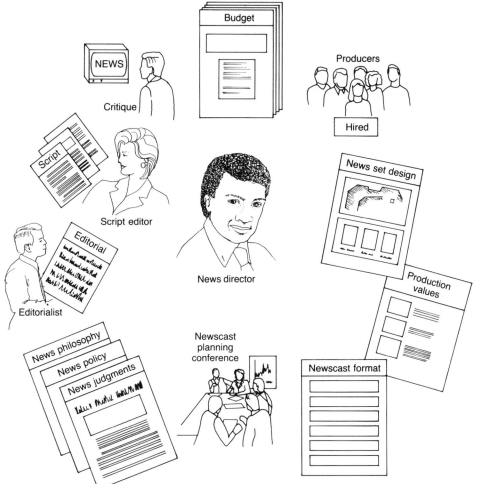

FIGURE 2–3
News director's responsibilities. The news director has ultimate control and responsibility for the newscast. That control and responsibility begins with the budget. The news director's role closes with a critique of the daily newscast.

the creation of the production values. (See the newscast design form.)

Creating and maintaining the newscast format (ND 5) The news director designs the format or order of program flow. Elements of news philosophy are reflected in a newscast format. The order of stories in a format reflects news values, the amount of time allotted to weather and sports conveys values, and the presence of an editorial in a newscast expresses values. The format may be one of the most important statements of a newscast. It is the responsibility of the news director to see that the producing staff maintain the format; in addition, the news director must approve any format change. (See the newscast format form.)

Auditioning and choosing newscast talent and editorialist (ND 6) The news director auditions and chooses the talent. The talent for a newscast may include the anchor(s), co-anchor(s), weathercaster, and sportscaster. Other on-air talent might include special correspondents, such as a medical reporter, legal and ethical reporter, or media reviewer. Auditions for the talent roles may be announced to the public and advertised in trade magazine classified sections or job information newsletters. Auditions for each applicant require a videotape sample of previous on-camera work as well as news writing samples. Photographs of applicants may also be requested. In-studio auditions may be required to test applicants in combination with others. The news director is responsible for the final choice of talent. An editorialist is one talent role that requires special attention. Some editorialists may be chosen from in-house personnel, often from television station management. Some salaried personnel may be expected to serve as editorialist by job description. (See the talent audition form.)

Managing the newsroom, news personnel, and news gathering sources (EP 1) The executive producer takes over the news and newsroom management from the news director on a day-to-day basis. The management responsibility involves the newsroom facility, all news producing staff, and all incoming news sources.

Being responsible for individual newscasts and their day-to-day details (EP 2) In contrast to the news director who is responsible for the continued existence of the newscast, the executive producer maintains the daily newscast. The executive producer is the top decision maker for daily choices regarding the newscast.

Creating individual newscast format, content, and order (EP 3) The specific responsibilities of the executive producer center around the format or rundown of the news program, the particular news stories for inclusion in any newscast, and the specific order in which the stories are included in each news program. Decisions of newscast format, news content, and order of presentation can reflect the basic philosophy of the news operation as articulated by the news director. (See the newscast format form.)

Keeping up on and being aware of news makers, news events, and potential news (AE 1) The assignment editor is the real ''news hound'' in the newsroom. To the assignment editor falls the responsibility to be current on all news, be well read in news from local and national newspapers and news magazines, read standard wire services, monitor newsroom scanners for local emergencies, and monitor both local and national television news programs.

Assigning news stories and keeping the news assignment board updated (AE 2) The assignment editor needs to break down the potential news stories for any newscast with awareness of available reporters/writers, feature producers, and studio talent. From the mix of potential news stories and available personnel, the assignment editor creates a daily assignment list for distribution at the daily newscast planning conference. Besides the assignment list, most newsrooms have a wall board with the content of the assignment list to monitor all stories and all assigned reporting and feature producing personnel. The assignment editor needs to keep the assignment board updated throughout the day. (See the newscast assignment form.)

Monitoring scanners for local emergencies, e.g., at fire departments and police stations (AE 3) The assignment editor is the source of the breaking local news events. The assignment editor keeps tabs on potential local news events from mailings and phone calls from local residents. Local fire and police radio scanners are continually monitored for emergencies in the local broadcast area. (See the emergency services call log form.)

Planning news coverage (AE 4) In addition to preparing and updating the news assignment form and the assignment board, the assignment editor has to plan for the future. The best news coverage requires future planning as well as daily planning. Long range assignments looking to ratings sweep periods in the market require foresight. A part of planning for the future is taking into consideration personnel availability.

Maintaining future files and news beat files (AE 5) Essential to an assignment editor's role is the maintenance of what is called *future files* or *news beats*. These files are collections of data recorded and filed physically in file folders or electronically in computer generated databases. These files contain background information that will be useful one day (e.g., future obituary packages of local political leaders) or a collection of news-making organizations that could be the source of a spokesperson one day for future news events. (See the news beat/future file form.)

Reporting to the executive producer (NP 1) The news producer is the executive producer's hands-on person in the newsroom. The news producer's role is to get the individual newscast produced: written, videotaped, edited, timed, and formatted. Communication—informing one another throughout the day—is crucial to a good working relationship between the news producer and the executive producer.

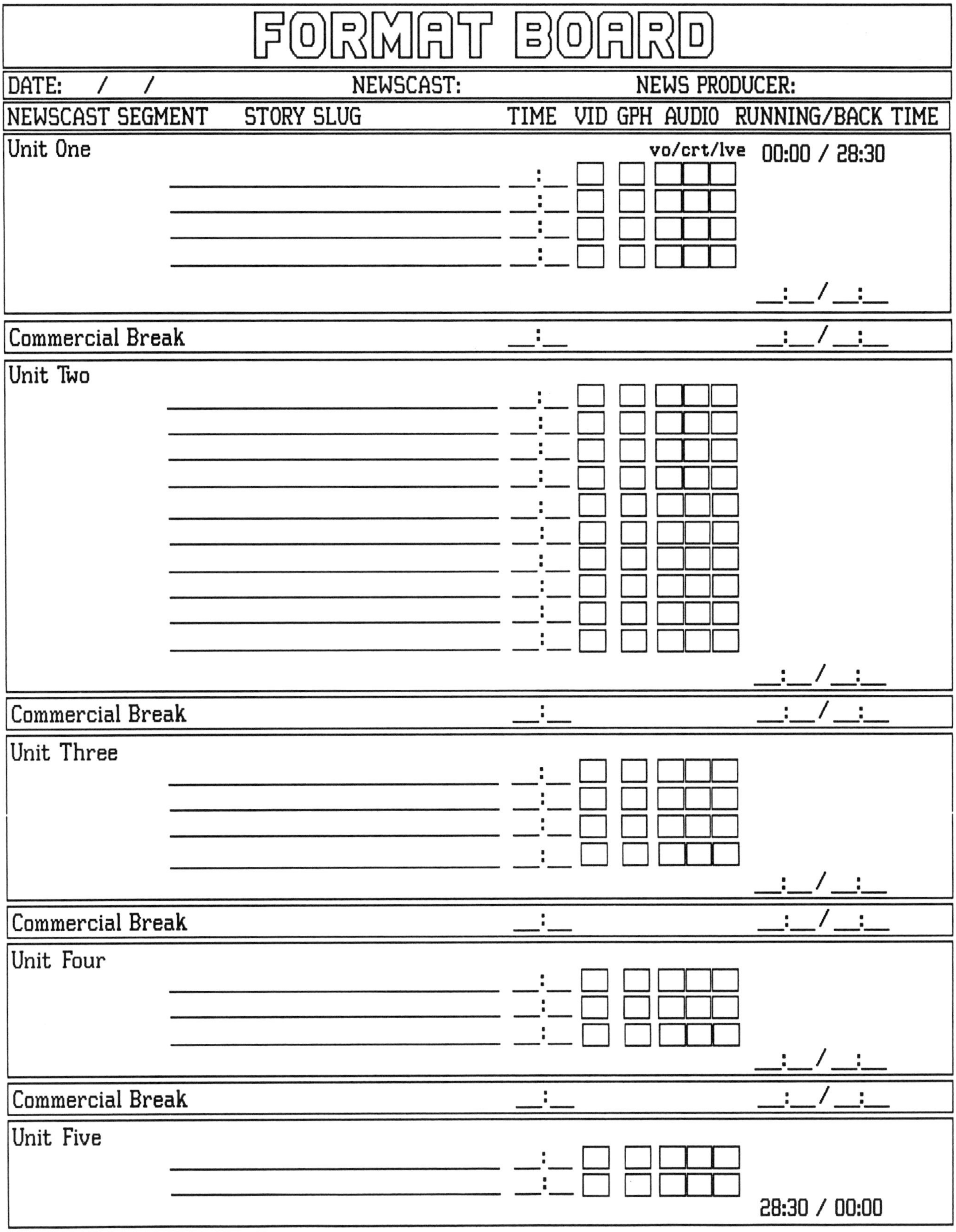

FORMAT BOARD

NEWSCAST SEGMENT	STORY SLUG	TIME	VID	GPH	AUDIO	RUNNING/BACK TIME

DATE: / /   **NEWSCAST:**   **NEWS PRODUCER:**

Unit One

vo/crt/lve 00:00 / 28:30

__:__ / __:__

Commercial Break   __:__   __:__ / __:__

Unit Two

__:__ / __:__

Commercial Break   __:__   __:__ / __:__

Unit Three

__:__ / __:__

Commercial Break   __:__   __:__ / __:__

Unit Four

__:__ / __:__

Commercial Break   __:__   __:__ / __:__

Unit Five

28:30 / 00:00

FIGURE 2–4
Newsroom format board. Newsrooms have write-on format boards on the wall for all to see and constantly update. Format boards are often hand-lettered, Plexiglas boards with felt-tip pens attached.

FIGURE 2–5
Executive producer's role. The executive producer serves as a manager and is often known as the assistant news director. The executive producer is a newsroom manager and decision maker.

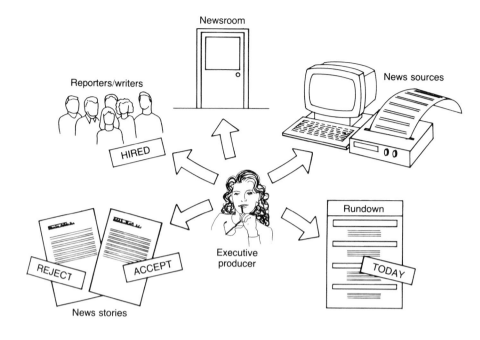

FIGURE 2–6
Assignment editor's role. The assignment editor performs the job assignment role for news producing. The assignment editor assigns stories, reporters, producers, videographers, and video editors. Keeping up on news is the single most important job of the assignment editor.

Working with the assignment editor (NP 2) As the hands-on work of the news producing staff is the responsibility of the news producer, a close working relationship has to exist between the news producer and the assignment editor. The assignment editor assigns news stories to reporters/writers and feature producers; the news producer monitors the reporters/writers and feature producers, facilitates the work, and gets it in on time.

Auditioning for and being chosen as newscast talent by the news director (T 1) Prospective talent—anchor, co-anchor, weathercaster, sportscaster, and special correspondents—apply and audition for positions. Openings for talent positions can be found in classified advertisement sections of trade magazines (e.g., in *Broadcasting Magazine*) and for job information newsletters (e.g., the Radio-Television News Directors Association newsletter).

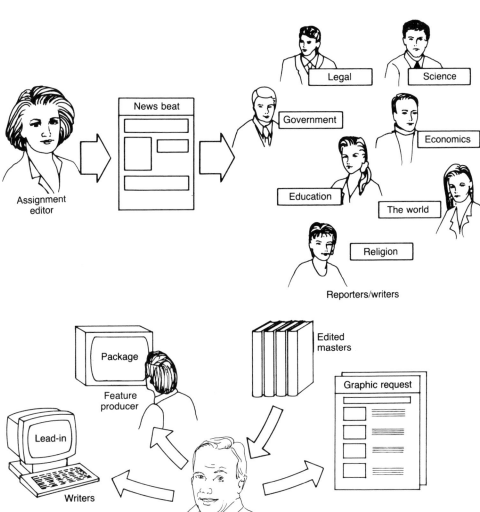

FIGURE 2–7
FIGURE 2–7
The news beat. The assignment editor assigns reporters and producers to their own beats. The beats become areas of expertise for the respective reporter or producer.

FIGURE 2–8
News producer's role. The news producer has to get the daily newscast produced; i.e., get the work done. The news producer works closely with the assignment editor, who assigns the work to be done.

Most talent applications require a videotape of previous on-camera work and samples of newswriting. Prospective talent may be asked to audition on-camera with other prospective talent. Applicants can expect to fill out forms requiring background information and provide a résumé or vita of previous employment. (See the talent audition form.)

Being chosen by the news director (E 1) Following the lead of most news media today, television newscasts increasingly include an editorialist among their on-air talent. The editorialist may be a member of the television station personnel, such as a general manager or a community relations officer. The editorialist is under the direction and approval of the news director.

Being hired or chosen by the executive producer (R/W 1) The executive producer hires or chooses reporters/writers to cover the news assigned to them. As reporters, they write their own gathered information into stories. They are also required to rewrite news copy from wire services. Reporters may become feature producers.

FIGURE 2–9
The role of the reporter/writer.
The reporter/writer begins the news producing day with an assignment from the assignment editor and follows it through to completion—at which time the completed story, edited master, and clipsheet are handed to the news producer.

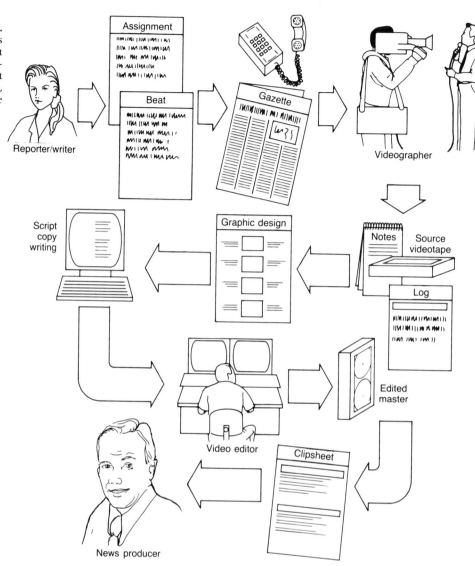

Reporters and feature producers must also have field reporting skills with the tact and responsibility to direct videographers, news makers, and video editors during the production of video news stories and feature packages. Some assigned news stories may be only readers for studio talent. A reader is a news story without any videotape to accompany it. A reader may or may not have a graphic.

Maintaining assigned beats (R/W 2) The practice in many news operations is to assign news beats to reporters/ writers. Each reporter is responsible for the assigned beat. A news beat is any specialized area of information that has potential news value. Examples of beats include education, medical, ethical, and legal areas. The reporter contacts and maintains a relationship with potential news makers within that beat. The beat relationship will be a source of news when events warrant news coverage or of in-depth coverage when the topic of the beat area is considered newsworthy (e.g., as during the production of a feature package). (See the news beat/future file form.)

Being hired or chosen by the executive producer (FP 1) Feature producers are hired or chosen by the

executive producer. Feature producers need the skills for producing longer video packages. These packages are usually soft news pieces and are generally produced on location over a longer period of time with a future deadline. The executive producer assigns feature producers from among skilled reporters/writers. A feature producer also may be a reporter/writer who took the initiative to propose a feature package. There are some feature producers hired only for the production of longer video packages.

Chairing the newscast planning conference for each newscast (ND 7) The newscast planning conference is the arena for beginning each newscast. For a daily newscast, the conference meets as early in the working day as possible to gather news producing personnel. The news director chairs the conference, reviewing the potential news stories of the day, suggesting the format order, monitoring assignments for that day and for future newscasts, making decisions on news stories, recommending news policy and newscast philosophy applications, and reviewing legal issues. The news director closes the conference.

Attending the newscast planning conference (EP 4)

The executive producer attends the planning conference in the role of ultimately being responsible to oversee the newsroom, news personnel, and news gathering sources related to the newscast being created.

Attending the newscast planning conference (AE 6)

The planning conference is the main forum for the assignment editor to organize and announce the news stories and personnel assignments for the newscast being created. The assignment editor presents local and national news and potential news events at the meeting. If the news assignment list has not already been distributed, the assignment editor distributes it at the conference. Changes may be made given the input and exchange of other producers during the conference. (See the newscast assignment form.)

Attending the newscast planning conference (NP 3)

The news producer attends the planning conference with an eye to what will have to be accomplished before the newscast is produced. The news producer must weigh the energies, equipment, resources, and time available to meet the decisions and assignments coming out of the conference.

Attending the newscast planning conference (R/W 3)

Reporters/writers attend the planning conference to offer input into news events of the day and to report on the progress of on-going assignments, often in the light of the beats for which they are responsible. The conference also is a valuable source of news story leads for reporters/writers.

Attending the newscast planning conference (FP 2)

Feature producers attend the planning conference as part of the staff of producers and reporters/writers. This meeting is the place for sharing insights, viewpoints, and news leads. Progress reports on feature packages may be required from producers.

Attending the newscast planning conference (E 2)

The editorialist attends the planning conference in preparation for the choice and discussion of the topic for an editorial. The collective experience and wisdom of newscast producers create an exciting forum for the development of the topic and direction of an editorial. It would not be uncommon for a special editorial board made up of television station personnel and news producers to reserve the choice of an editorial to themselves and not to the newscast planning conference.

Attending the newscast planning conference (T 2)

The anchor(s) and/or co-anchor(s) attend the newscast planning conference as the on-air representative(s) of the news organization or in additional roles as reporters/writers or feature producers. They are open to news assignments, location reporting, and feature producing. Their input about format, studio production, and future package series is very important to all supervising producers.

Receiving news assignments from the assignment editor (R/W 4)

At the planning conference, the reporters/writers receive their news assignments for the newscast being created. These assignments may be for a video news story or for a studio news reader only. They also receive the advice and direction of producers in the form of known leads and receive their assigned videographers and video editors. The planning conference is also the forum for the assignments of future feature packages.

Receiving a feature package assignment from the news producer or proposing a feature package/treatment to the news producer (FP 3)

The feature producer receives a feature package assignment at the planning conference. A feature producer (or reporter/writer) can take the initiative and write a proposal in the form of a treatment for a feature package. Feature packages can be a single unit assignment or a series assignment. (See the package treatment form.)

Researching the news assignment, following leads, and making phone calls (R/W 5)

With the conclusion of the newscast planning conference, the reporter/writer begins to cover the news assignment received. Leads from news sources, wire services, newspapers, and phone calls are followed. Once leads bear some fruit, appointments are made to get to news makers. Times and places are firmed up for videotaping. For fast breaking news, the reporter may just contact an assigned videographer and rush to the scene of the event. The ideal situation is to have adequate time to make appointments with news makers and communicate with an assigned videographer.

Researching the content of a feature package and following leads (FP 4)

The feature producer begins a package assignment by researching the topic. There may be future files available, leads from news sources, unsolicited phone calls, or ideas from newspapers and news magazines. Some of the best leads available are from colleagues.

Arranging the video shoot (R/W 6)

When there is lead time for a reporter/writer to cover an assigned news story without rushing, the video shoot is arranged by making appointments with news makers, communicating the details to an assigned videographer, and securing a news vehicle.

Making phone calls for appointments with news makers and prospective talent (FP 5)

Most leads are pursued by follow-up phone calls and appointments for in-person research or interviews with news makers and prospective on-camera talent.

Writing a treatment/proposal for a feature package (FP 6)

Many executive producers and news producers require a treatment from a feature producer before final approval of the project. This approval covers any expenses involved in the production of a feature package. The feature producer assigned a package will need the treatment before more time, personnel, equipment, and travel expenses are allotted. The treatment should follow adequate research by the feature producer on the topic of the package. When a feature producer initiates a feature package, the initiative is in the form of a treatment/

FIGURE 2–10
Feature package ideas. The ideas for a feature package come from many sources, including from the producer.

FIGURE 2–11
The process of feature package production. The feature producer has to follow a process of preproduction, production, and postproduction procedures in bringing a feature package to completion. Feature packages are long-term projects.

proposal and probably will not have to be redone. (See the package treatment form.)

Submitting a treatment/proposal for approval to the executive producer or news producer (FP 7) When the treatment/proposal is complete, the feature producer submits it to either the executive producer or news producer for approval.

Performing preproduction tasks: writing a preproduction script, creating the script breakdown, scouting location sites, and creating a camera shot list (FP 8) Upon receiving approval (perhaps with comments and suggestions from either the executive producer or the news producer or both) the feature producer performs the necessary preproduction tasks of a producer. First is preparation of the preproduction script. This script is based loosely on the research gained earlier. The preproduction script serves as a guideline for further producing and production. It should contain as many elements as possible of a finished package (e.g., interviewee names, interviewer questions, and proposed locations). Next, a script breakdown is created, which determines an order for location production. Preproduction scripts will be generally shot out of edited order for the time and convenience of videotaping. Once shooting order is determined, the producer may have to scout locations in the field for later videotaping. Then, with location site infor-

mation and the script breakdown at hand, the producer can design the shot list for the videographer. (These tasks and other details of the single camera shoot are described at length in my earlier book, *Single Camera Video: From Concept to Edited Master* [Focal Press, 1989].) (See the video script/storyboard form, script breakdown form, location site survey form, and remote camera shot list form.)

Accepting news reporting and feature producing assignments (T 3) Anchor(s) and/or co-anchor(s) receive news reporting and feature producing assignments in most news operations during the planning conference. Professional news consultants indicate that when the viewing audience sees the studio talent reporting from the field their credibility as on-air talent is increased.

Attending the newscast planning conference (D 1) It is helpful to the studio director to attend the planning conference. Often problems occurring in the control room and studio during production are a function of the producing staff. This is an opportunity for the studio director to encourage or limit video production values as part of package production of video news coverage. Having the studio director at this meeting affords the producers the opportunity to air their expectations of studio production techniques.

Setting a production schedule and making appointments with the news maker and talent and arranging the location shoot (FP 9) Having completed the preproduction tasks, the feature producer then creates a production schedule of times and dates for videotaping the news maker or prospective talent involved in the feature package production. Arranging the location shoot involves securing videotaping permission in some instances and making appointments with talent. (See the production schedule form.)

Being responsible for newscast philosophy and news judgments (ND 8) The planning conference is the primary forum for the news director to express and decide questions of the news operation's philosophy and policy regarding news content, coverage, and treatment. Part of the news philosophy and policy includes the legal ramifications, station liability, ethics of methods of news gathering, use of sources, and use of copyrighted material.

Being responsible for hard and soft news stories in the newscast (AE 7) The assignment editor continues, from the planning conference to studio production, to be ultimately responsible for all news content decisions, both hard and soft, for every newscast. When hard news or soft news stories change or fail to come together, the assignment editor is the final arbiter. This may mean consulting with the news director and news producer.

Overseeing the choice of an editorial (ND 9) After the choice of news stories and feature packages, the direct reflection of news philosophy and policy is in the choice of a topic for editorializing. As is the practice of newspapers and news magazines, an editorial has become part of most newscasts. Under the direction and approval of the news director, the planning conference (or station editorial board) suggests and develops those topics to be commented on by an editorialist.

Researching the assigned editorial (E 3) After the planning conference, the editorialist researches the chosen topic for the editorial as preparation to writing the editorial. Gathering related news sources, making clarifying phone calls, and contacting relevant experts or consultants become part of the dedication of the newscast staff and the editorialist to thoroughness and accuracy in presenting the opinion on the newscast.

Creating the hard news newscast format segment (AE 8) The assignment editor makes the inclusionary decisions (applying the newsworthiness criteria for including a news story in a newscast) and the exclusionary decisions (applying those criteria for deleting a news story in order to replace it with a newer one) throughout the day after the planning conference. These decisions mean

that a close working relationship must exist among the assignment editor, the news producer, and the news director. (See the newscast format form.)

Assigning videographers and keeping the videographer assignment board updated (AE 9) An outcome of reporter/writer and feature producer assignments during the planning conference is the assignment of videographers to the reporters/writers and feature producers needing or expecting to videotape in the field. As videographers receive their assignments, the assignment editor updates the master assignment board as a source of control of available personnel throughout the news preparation day. (See the remote assignment form.)

Being assigned by the assignment editor to a reporter or feature producer (VG 1) After the planning conference, videographers receive their assignments to those reporters/writers and feature producers who need videotaping done to complete their news assignments. The assignment editor logs and updates videographer assignments on the master assignment board in the newsroom.

Assigning video editors and keeping the video editor assignment board updated (AE 10) Another outcome of the planning conference is the assignment of videotape editors to reporters and feature producers to edit news stories and feature packages for telecast. As editors are assigned, the assignment editor updates the video editor and editing suite reservation board. This is an important way for the assignment editor and the news producer to monitor the progress of all video sources for the newscast. (See the editor/editing reservation form.)

Being assigned to a reporter or feature producer by the assignment editor (VE 1) If the reporters/writers or feature producers will not be doing the editing of the videotape for their own packages, the assignment editor assigns a video editor to the project. (See the editor/editing reservation form.)

Contacting the assigned videographer (R/W 7) Once a news story begins to come together and videotaping appointments are made with a news maker, the reporter/writer contacts the assigned videographer to plan the details of equipment reservation, news vehicle reservation, and appointment and travel time determination. If the story is fast breaking news, there may not be time for much preplanning, and rushing to the scene of the news event is paramount.

Contacting the assigned videographer and making travel plans (FP 10) The feature producer contacts the videographer assigned to the project as soon as a production schedule with talent and location is firm. Travel plans may have to be made. Most feature package productions involve travel for the videographer and producer.

Contacting the assigned video editor (R/W 8) As soon as the reporter/writer finalizes details of a video shoot with the assigned videographer, the reporter/writer confirms editing details with the assigned video editor. Editing details include expected length of edited video, time frame to begin editing, and any special editing effects expected.

Contacting the assigned video editor (FP 11)   The feature producer meets with the video editor assigned to the feature package. With the style of the feature package known and with some preproduction idea of the final look of the package, beginning editing details can be worked out in terms of date and time for editing, length of editing session(s), and expected special video effects.

Meeting with the assigned reporter or feature producer (VG 2)   After receiving an assignment, the videographer and reporter/writer or feature producer meet. To cover necessary videotaping, the reporter/writer or feature producer and videographer have to determine the extent of videotaping needed and set time and travel plans.

Meeting with the assigned reporter or feature producer (VE 2)   The video editor meets with the assigned reporter/writer or feature producer. Together they determine the necessary time frame to get the videotape for a news story or feature package edited.

Evaluating editing needs and requesting special effects hardware (VE 3)   Having determined the editing needs of the assigned reporter/writer or feature producer, the video editor decides what special effects will be required for editing. Once special effects are requested by a reporter/writer or feature producer, specific effects hardware may be needed (e.g., freeze frame, squeeze, or flip). Some of these special effects require control room switcher reservation in addition to normal editing suite use.

Reserving the video editing suite and updating the editing suite reservation board (VE 4)   As soon as videotape editing needs are finalized with the assigned reporter/writer or feature producer, the video editor reserves an editing suite for a given period of time. The

VIDEO EDITOR/EDITING SUITE RESERVATION BOARD

DATE: / /	NEWS ASSIGNMENT EDITOR:				NEWS PRODUCER:		
STORY/ FEATURE	REPORTER/PRODUCER	VIDEO EDITOR	EDITING SUITE	SPECIAL EFFECTS	SPECIAL INSTRUCTIONS	BEGIN SESSION	END SESSION
						: am/pm	: am/pm
						: am/pm	: am/pm
						: am/pm	: am/pm
						: am/pm	: am/pm
						: am/pm	: am/pm
						: am/pm	: am/pm
						: am/pm	: am/pm
						: am/pm	: am/pm
						: am/pm	: am/pm
						: am/pm	: am/pm
						: am/pm	: am/pm
						: am/pm	: am/pm
						: am/pm	: am/pm
						: am/pm	: am/pm
						: am/pm	: am/pm
						: am/pm	: am/pm
						: am/pm	: am/pm
						: am/pm	: am/pm

FIGURE 2–12
Video editor/editing suite reservation board. Most newsrooms use a wall board on which is logged the reservation of editing suites and video editors. These wall boards are often hand-lettered, Plexiglas boards and are written on with felt-tip pens.

REMOTE ASSIGNMENT BOARD

| DATE   /   / | | | | NEWS ASSIGNMENT EDITOR: | | | |

STORY/ FEATURE	REPORTER/PRODUCER	VIDEOGRAPHER	CAMERA UNIT	VEHICLE	DESTINATION	DEPART	RETURN
						: am pm	: am pm
						: am pm	: am pm
						: am pm	: am pm
						: am pm	: am pm
						: am pm	: am pm
						: am pm	: am pm
						: am pm	: am pm
						: am pm	: am pm
						: am pm	: am pm
						: am pm	: am pm
						: am pm	: am pm
						: am pm	: am pm
						: am pm	: am pm
						: am pm	: am pm
						: am pm	: am pm
						: am pm	: am pm
						: am pm	: am pm
						: am pm	: am pm
						: am pm	: am pm

FIGURE 2–13
Remote assignment board. Newsrooms must monitor and log all out-of-newsroom personnel. This is done with a wall board that tracks reporters, videographers, vehicles, and destinations. Departure and return times are also noted. These boards are mounted, hand-lettered, Plexiglas and are written on with felt-tip pens.

editing suite and time period should be recorded on the editing suite reservation board in the newsroom. Keeping this board updated as videotaping and editing plans change facilitates the efficient use of editing personnel and editing hardware. (See the editor/editing reservation form.)

Reserving remote video recording equipment and news vehicle (VG 3) Once a videographer receives an assignment and meets with the reporter or feature producer, the video recording equipment to be used must be noted on the remote assignment reservation board for the time required by the reporter/writer or feature producer. Some reservations for video recording equipment may be for future shoots on a remote location. The videographer also is responsible for reserving the news vehicle for location travel. (See the remote assignment form.)

Overseeing the production of all newscasts and keeping the newscast on the air (ND 10) With the end of the planning conference, the news director's primary

concern is for those details that involve the newscast in general and its continued production. The details include the application of news philosophy and policy; legal matters; budget; personnel; news sources; major purchases; and relationships with management, with the viewing audience, and with the local political community.

Overseeing program producers (EP 5) With the end of the planning conference, it is the responsibility of the executive producer to oversee all program producers by monitoring the progress of the elements of the format for the newscast. This entails frequent communication with the assignment editor for changes in the format and with the news producer for stages of completion of assigned video production.

Continuing to monitor newsroom scanners, wire service sources, and phone calls in order to update news story choices or add new stories (AE 11) The assignment editor has the responsibility to continue monitoring all incoming news sources for the purpose of staying on top of breaking news. With new information or new stories, decisions have to be made about changing the existing format at any point by adding to or changing assigned stories, by changing the length of time needed to cover a story, or by changing the order in which a story may be placed in the format. The assignment editor makes these decisions in consultation with the executive producer.

Making format decisions and changes throughout the news day (EP 6) Throughout the news preparation day, as the assignment editor monitors news sources, decisions have to be made about changes in the format for that newscast. Decisions involve new information or new stories, existing stories to be deleted, new stories to be added, length of time needed to cover stories, and placement order within the format. The executive producer makes these decisions in consultation with the assignment editor.

Reporting to and communicating with the news director (EP 7) The executive producer keeps the news director informed throughout the news day on changes and decisions affecting the format for the day's newscast. Major trouble-shooting should involve the combined roles of news director and executive producer.

Coordinating news stories for each newscast (NP 4) The news producer is responsible for coordinating the news stories for the daily newscast. This entails knowing where reporters/writers and feature producers and their videographers are at any time (i.e., traveling, on location, in the newsroom, or editing) as well as covering or completing news stories. Many news operations coordinate reporters/writers, producers, and videographers by beeper communication, two-way radio, cellular telephones, or by a system of reporting in by personnel via telephone throughout the day. This keeps the news producer updated on the progress of news coverage. The news producer consults the news assignment form and remote assignment form to keep track of the news stories and format.

Assigning graphics needs (NP 5) The news producer creates a list of graphics production needs for the graphic artist/producer once news stories are assigned. This permits the graphic artist/producer to begin graphics production for the newscast. The news director updates graphic designs and needs as reporters/writers and feature producers report in from the field. Deadlines have to be set for requesting graphics. (See the graphic design request form.)

Receiving requests for graphics from the news producer, reporters/writers, or feature producers (G 1) Early in the news preparation day, the news producer prepares a graphics request list from assigned news stories and distributes the list to the graphic artist/producer. The graphics request list is usually subject to change and may be added to as reporters/writers and feature producers report in throughout the news day.

Listing assigned stories and determining graphics needs (G 2) From the news producer's list of news stories and graphics requests, the graphic artist/producer determines the images and text for each graphic. Images and text may be part of a request or may be left to the discretion of the graphic artist/producer. In some cases, the graphic artist/producer will have to refer to the news story itself to determine the proper content of a graphic. (See the graphic design request form.)

Preparing and creating graphics (G 3) Once the content of a news story is clear and the imaging and text decided, the graphic artist/producer begins production of the requested graphics. Graphics production may entail creation of a graphic by artwork and 35mm photography for film slides; by computer graphic design and video transfer; or, simply, by choosing from a set of preproduced graphics, 35mm slides, video library, or still store memory.

Monitoring and reviewing all video for the newscast (NP 6) Throughout the news preparation day, the news producer keeps tabs on all stages of video production (i.e., videotaping and video editing) and reviews the final video products of video editors and producers from the edited master tape. The news producer makes the decision of acceptability of video quality and video editing for telecast. The news producer may require that a video piece be re-edited before airing.

Picking up remote video equipment and signing out the news vehicle (VG 4) The videographer is responsible for securing the reserved video equipment for the location shoot at the reserved time. The videographer also signs out the reserved news vehicle.

Securing source videotape stock for location recording (R/W 9) The reporter/writer is responsible for securing adequate source videotape cassette stock for video recording in the field.

Assisting the reporter/writer or feature producer on location (VG 5) As the videographer expects assistance from the reporter/writer or feature producer while on location, the videographer should expect to offer assistance when the reporter/writer or feature producer needs it. This may entail gaining access to a news maker, choosing shooting areas, suggesting better locations, or suggesting better shots.

Setting up the video camera, videotape recorder, lighting instruments, and audio microphones on location (VG 6) As the reporter/writer or feature producer begins contact with the news maker and prepares for the interview, the videographer sets up the video recording equipment. Many seasoned videographers have much of the video recording equipment set and readied in the news vehicle before departing for a shooting location or they assemble it while traveling. This is especially true for covering fast breaking news events. The videographer reviews the remote camera shot list prepared by the reporter/writer or feature producer for the shoot.

Producing and directing the location videotaping and interviewing talent (FP 12) The feature producer, given the nature of a feature package or series, takes strong producing and directing roles on location. The news maker or prospective talent needs to know what is required of him or her. Talent will want to know what questions are going to be asked. The feature producer may also have to handle nervous talent. The videographer needs to know what video is expected. The producer might review the shot list with the videographer. If a thorough preproduction script was created, storyboard frames may answer most of the videographer's questions. Most feature packages make use of interviews; hence, most producers serve as interviewers. When required (e.g., for controversial topics and underage children), the producer must have the talent sign the talent release form. (See the talent release form.)

Keeping a remote log (FP 13) A time saver for the feature producer is keeping a remote video log. The log consists of a running notation of all takes on location, the video and audio content of each take, videotape recorder counter reading for each take, and a comment on the good or bad qualities of the take. Taking the time to record this information in the field will lessen the time needed to view all source tape again to make the same notations later. (See the remote log form.)

Producing the video shoot, interviewing, collecting information (R/W 10) The reporter/writer produces the video shoot on location with the assigned videographer. This involves directing the videographer for the required video to cover the news story. Some of the most common video required for news stories is an interview with the news maker. The responsibility of the reporter/writer during the location shoot is to collect the necessary news information to enable the writing of the news copy to complete the news story. The reporter/writer may choose to do a location stand-up, which records the lead for the story; bridges or internal summaries, which allow the reporter to edit between interviewees throughout a news story; or a stand-up tag to the remote video coverage of the story. The criterion of adequate video coverage in the field is to shoot for the edit. A good reporter/writer plans the video coverage of a story from the time the assignment is made, traveling to the news event, collecting information, directing videotaping, and returning to the studio. At the conclusion of videotaping, the reporter/writer will have to obtain the news maker's signature on the talent release form in the case of a controversial topic or the use of underage children. (See the talent release form.)

Videotaping according to the directions of the reporter/writer or feature producer's directions (VG 7) The videographer is expected to follow the direction of the reporter/writer or feature producer responsible for the news story or feature package. A good working relationship permits the videographer to make suggestions to the reporter/writer or feature producer during the location shoot. The experienced eye of a videographer may see video opportunities that are missed by a reporter/writer or feature producer who is preoccupied with other details of a story or package and the talent.

Keeping a remote video log (R/W 11) A time saver in the field for the reporter/writer is keeping a remote log of all the video recorded on location. Every video take in the field should be noted on the log. Notations next to the

take should record the videotape recorder counter, indicate the content of the video, and comment on whether the video is good or bad and the reason for the judgment. The remote log will save valuable time in the newsroom and editing suite later by providing a log of all of the video shot on location and where it is on the source tape. Keeping a remote log saves having to review all of the source videotape later before choosing edit bites. (See the remote log form.)

Removing the record button from the source videotape and labeling the videocassette and case (VG 8) The protection of the videotape and its contents is the responsibility of the videographer. The first precaution against accidentally erasing or videotaping over recorded video is to remove the record button from the videocassette. Proper labeling of the videocassette and its case also ensures proper handling and recovery of the videotape before editing begins.

Assisting the videographer on location (FP 14) The feature producer should assist the videographer while on location. After completing location detail checks, including relations with the talent or news maker, the feature producer should be a part of equipment set-up. This holds for striking the shooting location also.

Assisting the videographer on location (R/W 12) In addition to meeting the news maker and preparing for an interview or news event coverage, which takes precedence, the reporter/writer should assist the videographer in the set-up of video recording equipment while on location. This holds true for striking the location also.

Striking the location (VG 9) When the reporter/writer or feature producer has satisfactorily completed the required videotaping for the news story or the feature package, the decision is made to strike the location. The videographer is responsible for striking the video recording equipment.

Returning to the newsroom with the videographer (FP 15) The feature producer returns with the videographer to the station and newsroom after completing the location shoot.

Returning to the newsroom and writing the news story (R/W 13) When the remote shooting is complete, the reporter/writer and videographer return to the newsroom. The reporter/writer then begins to write the copy for the news story based on the information gathered on location and the videotape made. A better estimate of editing suite reservation needs and actual editing time might now be made and changed on the editing suite reservation board.

Returning to the newsroom with the reporter/writer or feature producer (VG 10) The videographer returns to the newsroom with the reporter/writer or feature producer at the completion of remote location shooting.

Reporting return arrival to the assignment editor (VG 11) It is the videographer's responsibility to report the return arrival to the assignment editor. This will make the videographer available for another assignment.

Returning the remote video recording equipment and reporting damage, malfunctioning, and needed maintenance (VG 12)   At the end of the videographer's assignments, all remote video recording equipment has to be returned to the video equipment storage area and any damage that occurred or was noticed, any malfunctioning of the equipment, or any maintenance needs should be reported.

Writing the production script (FP 16)   The feature producer's next responsibility in feature package production is to write a production script. The production script builds on the preproduction script with the information gained during the location shoot and from the recorded video. At this stage, when considering audio sources for the package, copyright clearance will have to be sought. Copyright holders expect adequate lead time from feature producers in securing necessary rights. Most copyright holders expect requests to be made in writing by mail or by fax. Copyright holders know that feature producers had lead time to produce the whole package and that clearances have to be seen as part of that lead time. (See the television script form.)

Submitting the graphic design request form to the graphic artist/producer (FP 17)   As the production script takes shape, the feature producer now integrates graphics to make a stronger visual point or content clarification in the video package. These graphics have to be designed on a graphic design request form and submitted to the graphic artist/producer. (See the graphic design request form.)

Preparing the editing work sheet (FP 18)   The feature producer begins preparing for videotape editing of the package. The first step in that preparation is to either review the remote log form or view all source tapes from the location shoot and transcribe all of the video takes on a location source tape onto the editing work sheet. The remote log sheet substitutes for the editing work sheet if the information was thoroughly recorded. Should other tape sources be needed (e.g., video library videotapes), an editing work sheet will have to be created from them. Most videotape editors or their news operations require this preparation stage before editing can begin. One of the greatest wastes of editors' and editing suite time is unprepared feature producers. Without an editing work sheet, unprepared producers attempt to make editing decisions during editing sessions and frantically search source tapes for video bites. (See the editing work sheet form.)

Preparing editing cue sheets (FP 19)   From the editing work sheet, the remote log, and the production script, the feature producer can create the editing cue sheet. The editing cue sheet is a written format or rundown of the proposed edited master. Drawing from notations on the editing work sheet and log form, the feature producer builds the final edited master on paper. This step saves immeasurable time during editing and affords quality video design and creativity to the feature producer. (See the editing cue sheet form.)

Overseeing videotape editing with the video editor (FP 20)   Having met prearranged editing time for the reserved editing suite, the feature producer oversees the editing of the feature package video from the editing cue sheet with the video editor. Final decisions rest with the feature producer. A producer should be open to suggestions from an experienced editor.

Writing the editorial (E 4)   With the aid of experts and consultants on the topic assigned, the editorialist writes the editorial.

Submitting the editorial to the news director for approval (E 5)   Because the news director is responsible for all news philosophy, policy, and judgments in general, the editorialist submits the script copy of the editorial to the news director for editing and approval.

Editing and approving the editorial (ND 11)   Exercising responsibility over news philosophy, policy, and judgment, including all legal matters, the news director edits the editorial script received from the editorialist. The news director approves the content and style before sending the editorial to the script editor for final editing and typing into the newscast script.

Answering all responsible replies to editorials (E 6)   The editorialist answers all mailed replies to previous editorials according to the policy of the news organization. Some newscasts afford responsible repliers an opportunity to reply on the air. The editorialist, in consultation with and under the direction of the news director, arranges for videotaping the replies for B-roll playback into future newscast productions.

Reporting to and communicating with the news director (EP 7)   The executive producer keeps the news director informed throughout the day on changes and decisions affecting the format for the day's newscast. Major trouble-shooting should involve the news director and executive producer.

Completing the edited master clipsheet for the news producer (FP 21)   Upon completion of editing, the feature producer accurately times the edited master video of the feature package and completes the edited master clipsheet. The edited master clipsheet indicates to the news producer what character generator copy is to be matted on the video package and when it should appear matted through the control room switcher during B-roll into the newscast. (See the edited master clipsheet form.)

Turning the videotape master over to the news producer (FP 22)   The final step for the feature producer is to hand the edited videotape master over to the news producer with the edited master clipsheet for the feature package.

Functioning as managing editor (ND 12)   The news director takes the responsibility of managing editor of news copy both as personnel supervisor (e.g., reviewing writing skills and videotape editing) and as legal overseer (e.g., checking for libel and unethical judgments).

Coordinating edited videotape into the newscast (NP 7) As reporters/writers and feature producers finish their assigned news stories and video packages, the news producer coordinates and updates them into the newscast format.

Helping plan soft news, feature packages, and feature series with reporters/writers and producers (NP 8) The news producer is a valuable resource for reporters/ writers and feature producers. With a wealth of experience, the news producer is in a position to direct a reporter/writer or feature producer to news leads, videotaping and editing techniques, and production values to assist them in their assignments.

Monitoring the process of feature packages (NP 9) Given the importance of feature packages and, especially, feature series to future newscasts, the news producer is responsible for inquiring frequently of assigned feature producers about the progress of packages and for plotting the development of all assigned packages and series. News producers use a video production calendar board to plot the progress of feature packages. (See the video production calendar form.)

Keeping the newscast program format board updated (NP 10) Because the news producer is responsible for

ensuring completion of daily assignments, the news producer is best capable of updating the format board throughout the day. Stories written and video edited are noted with their times of completion on the format board.

Being hired or chosen by the executive producer (SE 1) A script editor is used in larger news operations to oversee editing of a final studio production script. With many reporters/writers and feature producers submitting completed scripts throughout the day, some control and order is necessary. A single script editor creates a unified writing style, sentence length, and word choice to the final draft of the production script.

Indicating or confirming graphic production needs (R/W 14) As reporters/writers work their news stories to completion, they indicate new or changed graphics needs or confirm what was already requested from the graphic artist/producer. This can be done by reviewing the graphic design request list developed by the news producer and now in the hands of the graphic artist/ producer.

Submitting scripts of reader stories or voice-over video copy to the script editor (R/W 15) The reporter/ writer submits all scripts of assigned news readers or voice-over video script copy to the script editor for editing.

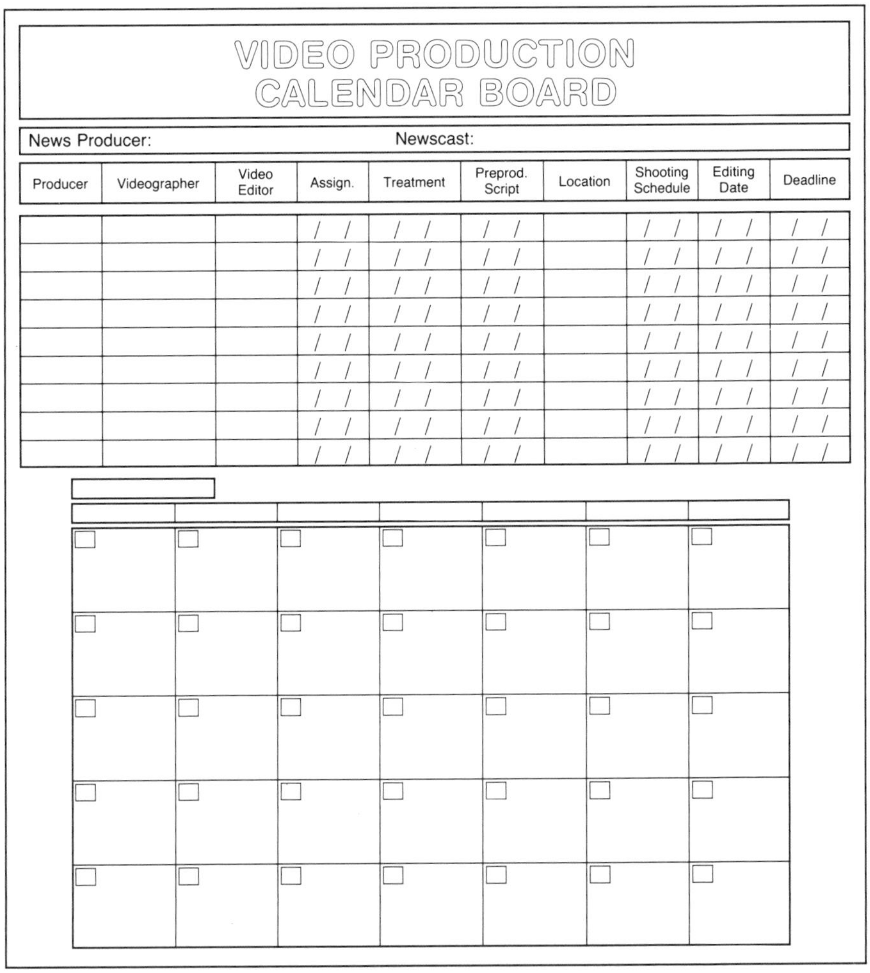

FIGURE 2–14
Video production calendar board. News producers require a system of monitoring and tracking long range video packages. A newsroom wall board logs producer, videographer, video editor, and stages of production of video packages. These wall boards are hand-lettered, Plexiglas and are written on with felt-tip pens.

Reading and editing all script copy before the final script is typed for the teleprompter (SE 2) The script editor reads all script copy not only in preparation for typing the studio production script for the teleprompter but to edit for writing style and form. In some news operations, reporters and producers type their own script for the teleprompter, with or without supervisory editing.

Typing the edited news story for the teleprompter (R/W 16) If the assigned news story for the reporter/ writer is a talent reader (i.e., to be read live from the studio during newscast production), the reporter/writer types the final draft of the edited script for the teleprompter.

Monitoring the newscast script from the reporter/ writer to the teleprompter (SE 3) The script editor monitors all drafts of script copy from the final writing stages to the studio teleprompter copy.

Doing voice-over recording from edited script copy (R/W 17) If the assigned story is a video piece, the reporter/writer records any voice-over audio track required for the video news story before the editing session.

Writing the studio talent lead-ins for video packages (NP 11) The news producer writes all studio talent lead-ins to the video packages as they are completed for the telecast. Edited master clipsheet forms contain some producer suggested lead-ins, but, as the script editor provides a single writing style for the content and form of the script, the news producer provides a unified style and mind set to the content of video package lead-ins.

Reviewing the editing cue sheets with reporters/ writers and feature producers prior to editing sessions (VE 5) Before going into an editing session, the video editor reviews the editing cue sheet from the reporter/ writer or feature producer to whom the video editor was assigned. The editing cue sheet is similar to a format/ rundown sheet for the newscast—it is the format or rundown for the videotape to be edited.

Reporting the completed graphics summary list to the news producer (G 4) By this time in the newscast preparation day, the graphic artist/producer has completed the requested graphics. The graphic artist/producer distributes those graphics that are to be inserted into preproduced video. The graphics slated for studio talent readers are put into format order on the graphics summary list for the news producer. (See the graphics summary rundown form.)

Distributing graphics sources and the summary list to the assistant director, technical director, telecine operator, and videotape operator (G 5) Because some graphics may be generated from different sources (e.g., 35mm film to the telecine, computer graphics from the still store, or freeze frame video from videotape playback) the graphic artist/producer provides a video sources list to those personnel who need it during studio production. (See the video sources form.)

Editing and overseeing videotape editing with the video editor (R/W 18) The reporter/writer meets the prearranged editing suite reservation time and either edits the video news story or oversees the videotape editing by the video editor. The reporter/writer comes to the editing session prepared with the editing cue sheet and all video and videotape dubs of audio sources necessary for the editing session.

Editing with the reporter/writer or feature producer (VE 6) The video editor edits the video news story with the reporter/writer or feature producer.

Deferring final editing decisions to the reporter/ writer or feature producer (VE 7) The video editor follows the directions of the reporter/writer or feature producer during editing. An experienced editor should feel free to make editing suggestions. Ultimately, the video editor defers final editing decisions to the reporter/ writer or feature producer.

Correcting video and audio levels and mixing audio tracks (VE 8) The video editor is responsible for the video quality of the final edited master—given acceptable source audio and video quality from the start. Correcting audio and video requires using a vectorscope to maintain video levels and filtering and equalizing audio inputs. Before editing is complete, the video editor must master the video piece by mixing the two audio tracks into one.

Removing the record button from the edited master and labeling the videocassette and its case (VE 9) The final task of the video editor, before handing the edited master over to the reporter/writer or feature producer, is to remove the record button from the cassette and properly label both the videocassette and the cassette's case.

Completing the edited master clipsheet for the news producer (R/W 19) The reporter/writer must take the edited master tape from the video editor and complete the clipsheet for the master tape. The clipsheet contains the timing of the video piece, a suggested lead-in, all accurate character generator copy to be matted over the video during production, and the times into the video piece at which the character generator copy should appear.

Submitting the master videotape and the clipsheet to the news producer (R/W 20) The final task for the reporter/writer is to turn over the edited master videotape and its clipsheet to the news producer for review and logging into the format.

Timing the newscast from the updated format (NP 12) As news reader scripts are edited and typed and video stories and feature packages completed and turned in with clipsheets, the news producer times the newscast from the updated format board. Timing includes all news stories, video pieces and packages, their lead-ins, studio talent banter copy, and any commercial breaks.

Creating a hand copy of the format and copying and distributing the final format/rundown sheet (NP 13) The news producer begins to close the preproduction stage by creating a hand copy of the updated format board. This format/rundown sheet has to be copied and distributed to those production crew members who need that information in studio production.

Creating the character generator copy master list for the production assistant (NP 14) The news producer has the responsibility at this final stage of preproduction to create a master character generator copy list from the reporter/writer and feature producer clipsheets and format board. The character generator copy master list must contain all character generator copy that is to appear matted on the screen during the newscast. This copy includes all talent lower thirds; film and video source credits; actuality lower thirds; and any transcriptions, trades, and closing credits.

Turning over all videotape masters and any film sources to the telecine operator and the videotape operator (NP 15) As a last preproduction step for the news producer, the news producer must turn over all videotape masters to the videotape operator and all film sources to the telecine operator.

Reviewing the format/rundown sheet from the format board or from the news producer's copy (SE 4) The script editor needs to keep constant track of the order of news stories and video pieces and packages for the newscast. The primary source for that information is the newscast format board or the format/rundown sheet.

Typing the remaining script copy for the teleprompter (SE 5) As all elements of the script come together, the script editor is responsible for completing the typing of the script for the teleprompter.

Printing and providing copies of the newscast production script (SE 6) The script editor must print the script and make multiple copies of it. When the final script is printed, multiple carbon copies are often made simultaneously.

Distributing copies of the newscast production script (SE 7) The script editor has the final responsibility to distribute the script copies to the studio talent, the teleprompter operator, and the studio director.

Supervising the studio production crew (D 2) The studio director is responsible for supervising all studio production crew. Supervision includes appointing the time and place for crew call before each newscast production and holding a production meeting with the production crew when necessary.

Reviewing and approving the audio and lighting design plots (D 3) The studio director oversees the creative aspects of the newscast production by reviewing the audio director's audio plot design and the lighting director's lighting plot design for the studio news set. The studio director reviews the plots, makes any necessary changes or suggestions, and approves the designs.

Securing a copy of the format/rundown sheet from the news producer and a copy of the script from the script editor (D 4) Two documents essential to the studio director are the format/rundown sheet and the

production script. A copy of the format/rundown sheet is available from the news producer and a copy of the script is available from the script editor.

Reviewing and studying the format/rundown sheet (D 5) The studio director becomes familiar with the format/rundown sheet. It must never be taken for granted that the format has not been changed.

Working on and preparing the script (D 6) Paramount to the preproduction tasks of the studio director is the time the studio director spends working over the script. Working with the format/rundown sheet, the studio director pages through the script coordinating the script to the format/rundown sheet and making directorial notations in the margin of the script to draw attention to important cues during production.

Creating the studio camera blocking plot and shot list (D 7) The studio director creates a camera blocking plot for the production. The camera blocking plot places the studio cameras in relation to the studio news set and studio talent who must be shot on-camera. Once the camera blocking plot is created it is rarely changed; however, changes in format, adding or subtracting talent from the newscast, or adding or altering the news set demand a new camera blocking plot. When the blocking plot is complete, the director breaks down the camera shots for the respective cameras and creates a shot list for each camera operator. (See the studio camera blocking plot form, studio camera shot list form.)

Scheduling crew call for each newscast and holding a production meeting with the studio crew when necessary (D 8) The studio director exercises control

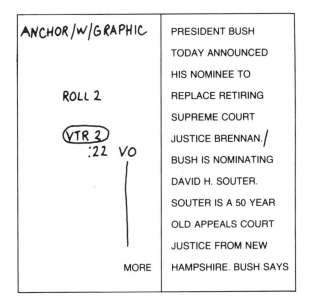

FIGURE 2–15
Sample of marked studio director's script. The studio director has to mark a copy of the script for studio directing. Marking notes changes in talent, use of video sources, length of video inserts, and cues in the script copy for changes.

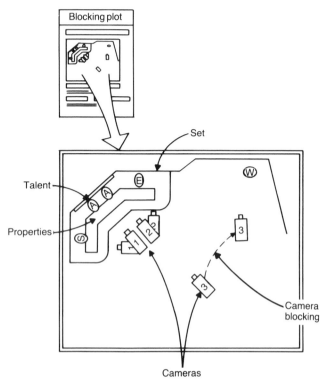

FIGURE 2–16
The studio director's blocking plot. Blocking the cameras for the newscast is usually a one time task. A new blocking plot is done if the set is changed, talent is reblocked, or the format is changed.

and direction over the studio production crew by scheduling the time and place for the crew call. The crew call is a rallying time for the studio production crew to assemble and complete preproduction tasks and begin production responsibilities.

When necessary, the studio director schedules and holds a production meeting. A production meeting is not important before every newscast, but should be held often enough to facilitate good working relationships among the crew and, more importantly, to create a good newscast. The production meeting is a forum for trouble-shooting production elements as well as applauding good production skills.

Being appointed by the studio director (AD 1) The relationship between the studio director and the assistant director is so close that the studio director chooses and appoints the assistant director to serve the studio director before and during production.

Reviewing and studying the format/rundown sheet (AD 2) The assistant director best serves the director in preproduction by becoming familiar with the format/rundown sheet.

Meeting with the assistant director (D 9) The studio director meets with the assistant director as part of preproduction responsibilities. The director conveys the studio director's expectations of the assistant director before (e.g., checking character generator copy and setting

timers and clocks), during (e.g., remote control of video sources and telecine), and after (e.g., control room strike and postproduction preparations) production.

Meeting with the studio director (AD 3) The assistant director needs time with the studio director as part of preproduction responsibilities. The assistant director requires some knowledge of what the director plans and needs before, during, and after studio production.

Reviewing and studying the format/rundown sheet (TD 1) The technical director reviews the format/rundown sheet as part of preproduction responsibilities. The technical director will have to preset the switcher effects in terms of the order and extent of any special production switcher effects.

Checking with the videotape operator and the video engineer (TD 2) The technical director needs to have good communication with both the videotape operator and the video engineer. The videotape operator assigns video playback sources that have to be routed through the switcher. The video engineer controls the camera signals that also have to be assigned and routed through the production switcher.

Updating the video sources checklist (TD 3) The technical director constantly checks for any changes in video sources needed for the newscast. The primary list of video sources and their playback and record deck assignment is the video sources form from the videotape operator.

Checking videotape playback and record monitors (TD 4) Besides videotape playback assignment and switcher routing, the technical director needs to be aware of the monitor assignment of those playback and record decks among the monitors that face the control room directing staff.

Reviewing and studying format/rundown sheet (PA 1) The production assistant relies on the format/rundown sheet not only during the remaining preproduction time but also during newscast production. Time is needed to review and become familiar with the format/rundown sheet.

Securing the character generator master list from the news director (PA 2) The production assistant secures the character generator master list as part of preproduction tasks. The news producer is responsible for preparing the character generator master list and turning over that list to the production assistant.

Beginning to enter character generator copy for the newscast (PA 3) Entering character generator copy into the character generator is an important preproduction task for the production assistant. Newscasts make abundant use of text on the screen. Accuracy of the content of the text reflects greatly on the credibility of the newscast.

Reviewing and studying the format/rundown sheet (A 1) The audio director begins preproduction tasks by reviewing the format/rundown sheet and becoming familiar with it. The order of news elements and the source of all audio components are noted from the format/rundown sheet.

Creating and getting approval for the audio plot design (A 2) The audio director creates the audio plot design considering the needs of the talent in the set and their movement. An audio plot will generally remain the same across the production of newscasts, but the audio director remains vigilant to any changes to the format from the format/rundown sheet for each newscast, which may require audio pick-up changes. The audio director submits the audio plot to the studio director for approval. (See the news set audio plot form.)

Beginning to set out microphones to be used for the newscast (A 3) Before the studio becomes busy, the audio director takes preproduction time to begin setting out microphones on the set. Microphone cable runs are chosen to avoid heavy personnel (e.g., talent and studio crew) and hardware (e.g., studio cameras and prompter bed) traffic patterns in the studio and on the set.

Securing prerecorded audio recordings and transferring to cartridges (A 4) The audio director determines from the format/rundown sheet what audio sources are not wedded to video and will require control from the audio control area of the control room. This necessitates transferring the audio recording to cartridges and cuing up if it has not already been done.

Checking all sound recorded sources and cuing the sources (A 5) The audio director takes an audio check on all recorded sound sources to be used in the newscast, which are under the control of the audio director, and cues up each source. Cuing the recorded source also involves setting gain, equalization, and tone levels for each source.

Reviewing and studying the format/rundown sheet (F 1) The floor director controls and directs many individuals in the studio during production, so the floor director must become very familiar with the format/rundown sheet. However, the format/rundown sheet is

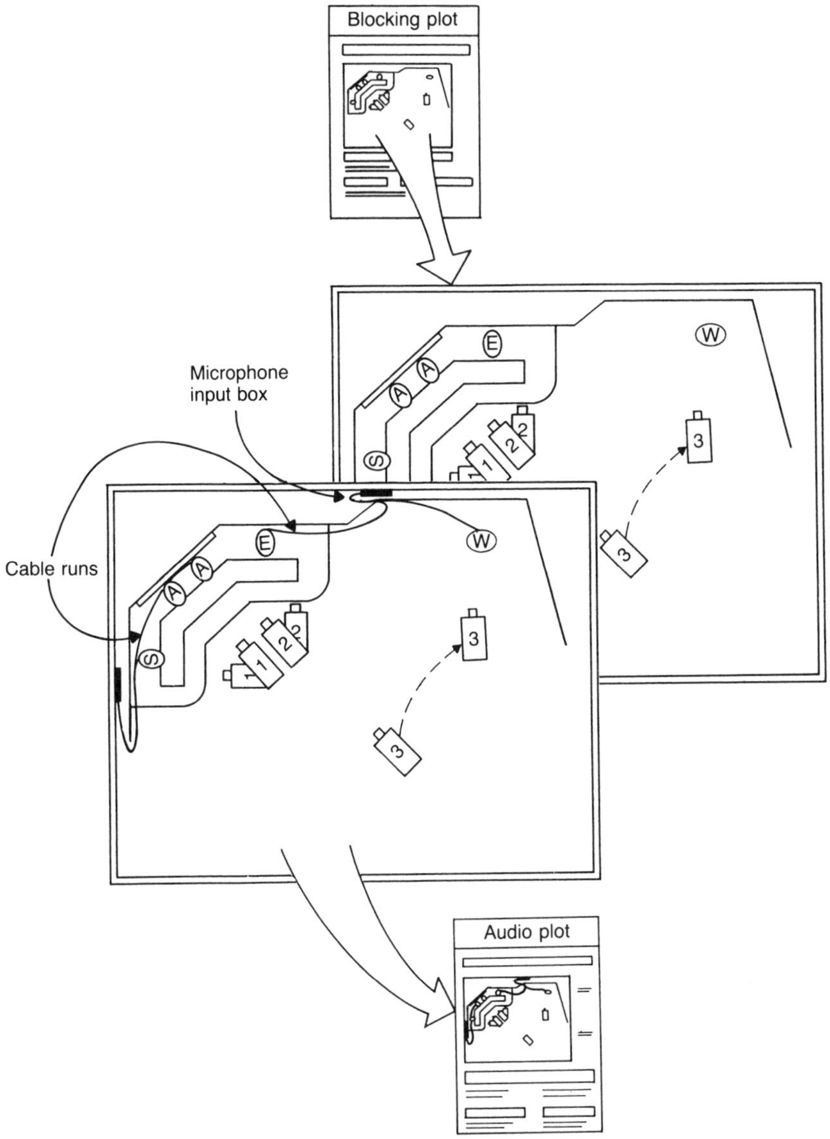

FIGURE 2–17
The audio plot. The audio director creates a blocking plot for the set. If the set is changed (e.g., new talent added), a new plot will be made.

readily available for reference to the floor director during production.

Beginning to set up the studio set and organizing the set (F 2)   The floor director functions as a stage manager for the production of the newscast. This means that all details of the set are attended to and readied for the talent and crew. All set properties (e.g., chairs or coffee tables) must be spotted on their spike marks.

Reviewing the format/rundown sheet for production order (TO 1)   The teleprompter operator requires a copy of the format/rundown sheet in order to become familiar with the final order of all elements of the newscast, including news stories involving use of the script. The teleprompter operator needs to review and study the format/rundown sheet as a prelude to setting up the teleprompter bed for the script.

Setting up the teleprompter bed (TO 2)   Setting up the teleprompter bed usually requires retrieving it from some other production area, checking all cable connections, setting the teleprompter camera lens and focus, and checking the teleprompter monitor for the reproduction of any text.

Securing the teleprompter script copy from the script editor (TO 3)   The teleprompter operator has to secure the prompter copy of the script. The script editor is responsible for preparing the final draft of the script, printing the script, and providing the necessary copies of the script, including the copy to the teleprompter.

Preparing to run the script copy for camera monitor text (TO 4)   Having secured the teleprompter copy of the script, the teleprompter operator must prepare the script for the teleprompter bed and check for transmission to the camera monitors.

Reviewing the format/rundown sheet (CO 1)   The camera operators prepare for production by reviewing and becoming familiar with the format/rundown sheet. The camera operators have ready reference to the format/rundown sheet by attaching the sheet to the clipboard at the rear of their cameras. The format/rundown sheet is thus always available to them.

Reviewing the camera shot list (CO 2)   The camera operators review the shot list of their own camera shots. The studio director creates the shot lists from the camera blocking plot as determined by the format/rundown sheet and by noting any changes to the production. The studio director distributes the shot lists to the camera operators during preproduction set-up or at crew call.

Checking the cameras for operation (CO 3)   The camera operators are responsible for retrieving their cameras from other areas of the studio, drawing adequate length of camera cable behind the cameras to facilitate camera movement during production, and doing a fast run through basic operation of the cameras. The video engineer assists with the camera check.

Choosing camera lens filter(s) (CO 4)   In some newscast productions, a very common production value requires a camera shot that includes studio lights in the framing. To guard against burning out sensitive camera tubes, a star filter, which will diffuse the strong studio light, is chosen and placed in front of each camera's lens. This filter and any other that may create a requested visual effect must be chosen during preproduction.

Balancing the pedestal of the camera (CO 5)   Another preproduction responsibility for the studio camera operators is to check the proper weight balance of the cameras' pedestals. Some studio cameras require counter weights against air pressure in the base of the pedestal to properly raise them up and down during production. Whatever the mechanical mode of pedestaling cameras, it has to be checked for fluid movement and preset to acceptable height.

Adjusting the handles of the studio camera (CO 6)   Many studio cameras have zoom and focusing handles that require adjusting to the comfortable arm and hand height of the individual camera operator. These have to be preset during preproduction.

Setting camera pan and tilt friction tension (CO 7)   Camera operators need to preset the degree of friction tension of panning and tilting mechanisms of the cameras. Too tight tension can create a jerky pan or tilt movement;

FIGURE 2–18
The studio prompter system. The prompter system runs the script under a light and a video camera lens and reproduces the script on a monitor attached to the front of each studio camera. The talent can read the copy from a reflection off glass in front of the camera's lens.

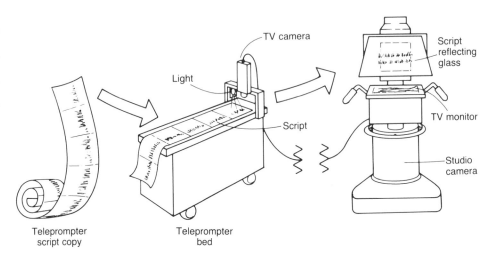

Teleprompter
script copy

Teleprompter
bed

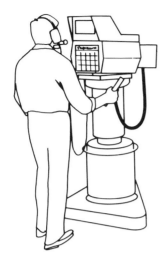

FIGURE 2–19
Using the shot list. Each camera operator places the appropriate shot list on the clipboard at the rear of the camera.

too loose tension can create a loss of control during panning and tilting.

Selecting the external video option for the camera monitor during production (CO 8) A final preproduction choice for camera operators is the choice, where available, of the external video line to the camera monitors. In newscast production, camera operators want to be able to see switcher-matted inserts in the program line to best help them frame live studio talent during video matte effects. The external video line choice for the camera monitors facilitates that visual convenience. It also affords the camera operators the opportunity to view external video sources in the newscast and permits them to be ready when the director signals a return to the studio cameras for video.

Reviewing the format/rundown sheet (TC 1) The telecine operator reviews and studies the newscast format/rundown sheet as a final check on the order of film sources for the newscast.

Securing all film sources from the news producer or graphic artist/producer (TC 2) As the videotape operator needs to secure all video sources for the newscast, the telecine operator must secure all film sources required for the newscast. The telecine is the source for 35 mm and 16 mm film in television production. The graphic artist/producer is responsible for having any 35mm slides required for the newscast; the news producer would have the same responsibility for any 16mm film planned for the newscast.

Designing and getting approval for the lighting plot for the set (LD 1) The lighting director is responsible for preparing the lighting design. The lighting director designs the lighting plot for the set and submits it to the director for approval. Upon approval, the set is lit and the design checked. Generally the design is checked by the lighting director, who walks the studio set with the lighting plot in hand and makes sure that all planned lights are operative. (See the news set lighting plot form.)

Adjusting and aiming lights and making light intensity adjustments for talent hair and clothes (LD 2) The lighting director makes specific adjustments to the lights after the talent are in place. Lighting instrument aiming, focusing, and intensity adjustments may have to be made with changes in talent, talent hair color or style, and talent wardrobe.

Checking the operation of video recorders and playback units (VTRO 1) The videotape recorder operator has the preproduction responsibility to check the operation of record or playback videotape decks for proper record and playback quality.

Performing preventive maintenance on videotape decks (VTRO 2) The videotape recorder operator performs regular preproduction maintenance on videotape decks. The very simple procedure of cleaning the recording and playback heads should be done before each newscast.

Checking the format/rundown sheet for video playback requirements during production as well as the order of playback (VTRO 3) The first forum from which the videotape recorder operator will determine video playback requirements is the format/rundown sheet. This will have to be reviewed during preproduction and in preparation for securing the master videotapes for the newscast.

Securing the master videotapes for A-roll and B-roll from the news producer (VTRO 4) The videotape recorder operator secures the master videotapes for playback into the newscast from the news producer. The alternating playback set-up required for A-rolling and B-rolling into the newscast can be determined from the format/rundown sheet.

Preparing A-roll and B-roll video dubbing (VTRO 5) With the master videotapes and the format/rundown sheet in hand, the videotape recorder operator can determine the alternating A-roll and B-roll playback requirements. The alternating playback requirements in turn require dubbing master videotapes back-to-back onto two separate videotapes in preparation for alternating A-roll and B-roll video playback into the newscast.

Choosing videotape playback and videotape record decks and alerting the technical director to the assignment (VTRO 6) Once the order of alternating playback and record videotape deck requirements is set by the videotape recorder operator, the technical director should be informed of the videotape deck assignments for routing through the control room switcher and monitors.

Checking the studio cameras with the camera operators (VEG 1) The video engineer is responsible for turning the cameras on and checking the cameras with the camera operators. Checking the camera includes back focusing, external video input choice, tally light operation, lens filter choice, etc.

Doing preventive maintenance on the cameras (VEG 2) During studio camera check is the opportunity for the video engineer to perform preventive maintenance on the cameras.

Checking the teleprompter monitors on the studio cameras (VEG 3)   The video engineer should take the time during preproduction to check the proper functioning and adjustments of the prompter monitors on the front of the studio cameras.

Uncapping the camera lenses (VEG 4)   The video engineer decides, when the cameras are safely locked down or in the hands of the camera operators, that the camera lenses can be uncapped.

Setting video levels and lens apertures with studio lights (VEG 5)   With lenses uncapped, the cameras locked down and focused on the same text area, and the studio lights at production intensity levels, the video engineer can set the video levels and choose a lens aperture setting for each camera. These are the settings that the video engineer will monitor throughout the newscast.

Routing the external video signal to camera monitors for camera operator use during production (VEG 6)   The video engineer takes the responsibility of routing the external video signal from the control room to the cameras. This external signal allows the camera operators to choose to monitor the control room program line to facilitate talent framing during production.

Checking tally light operation of cameras (VEG 7)   The video engineer takes preproduction time to check the operation of tally lights on the studio cameras. Many studio cameras permit tally lights to be turned off for some studio productions. On the other hand, newscast talent performance requires taking cues from the tally lights on cameras.

Meeting crew call for each newscast and attending the production meeting when scheduled (AD 4)   The assistant director completes preproduction assignments and responsibilities and meets crew call with other production crew personnel prior to production. The assistant director is also required to attend scheduled production meetings.

Meeting crew call for each newscast and attending the production meeting when scheduled (TD 5)   The technical director finishes preproduction responsibilities and meets with the director and other production crew members for crew call prior to production. The technical director also attends scheduled production meetings called by the studio director.

Meeting crew call for each newscast and attending production meetings when scheduled (PA 4)   The production assistant completes preproduction character generator copy inputting to meet with the studio director and other production crew members prior to studio production. The production assistant attends scheduled production meetings.

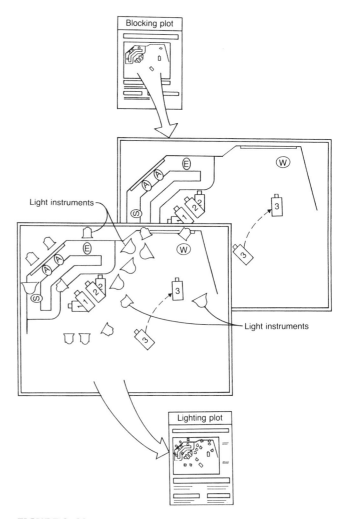

FIGURE 2–20
The lighting plot. The lighting plot need be designed only once. It will be referred to often to check and replace lights. If the set or talent are changed, the plot will have to be altered to accommodate the changes.

Meeting crew call for each newscast and attending the production meeting when scheduled (A 6)   The audio director completes preproduction responsibilities and set-ups and meets with the studio director and crew prior to production. A scheduled production meeting requires the attendance of the audio director.

Meeting crew call for each newscast and attending the production meeting when scheduled (F 3)   The floor director ends preproduction tasks by meeting with the studio director and production crew for crew call. This is the opportunity for the floor director to announce any studio or set changes. The floor director attends scheduled production meetings.

Meeting crew call for each newscast and attending the production meeting when scheduled (TO 5)   The prompter operator completes preproduction tasks by meeting crew call with the studio director and other crew

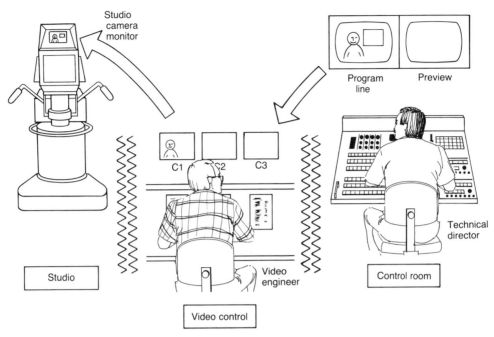

FIGURE 2–21
Routing the external video signal. The external video signal is the video signal from the control room line. Routing this to the studio cameras permits the camera operators to see the framing of the other cameras as well as the composite matted video images.

members. The prompter operator also attends all scheduled production meetings.

Meeting crew call for each newscast and attending the production meeting when scheduled (CO 9) The camera operators halt preproduction tasks by meeting with the studio director and other crew members for crew call. The camera operators are required to attend any scheduled production meetings.

Meeting crew call for each newscast and attending production meeting when scheduled (TC 3) The telecine operator meets with the studio director and production crew for crew call. The telecine operator is required to attend any scheduled production meetings.

Meeting crew call for each newscast and attending the production meeting when scheduled (LD 3) The lighting director ends preproduction by meeting with the studio director and other crew members for crew call. The lighting director attends scheduled production meetings.

Reviewing and critiquing newscast with personnel (ND 13) The news director has the on-going responsibility to review recent newscasts by way of videotape. The news director then offers critiques of the production to personnel within the operation to whom the criticism is directed. It would not be uncommon for a news director to review the most recent newscast as part of each newscast planning conference.

THE PRODUCTION PROCESS

The television newscast production is one of a small number of fully scripted video genres. Others include television studio drama production and television studio commercial production. Television news is not normally thought of as a fully scripted program in the manner we perceive drama, but the newscast is indeed fully scripted. Hence, the process of studio production of news takes on a stress and frustration level that is unexpected from first time observers. The reality of so much structured preproduction and the creation of a fully scripted format generates the tension that is often experienced in the control room and studio during production.

Newscast production involves the large studio production support crew common to any studio production. An average of 14 production staff (excluding talent and producers) occupy the control room, studio, audio booth (if separate from the control room), and master control area (where the videotape record and playback decks and telecine are located). If the newscast telecasts live, then additional staff is involved at the break switcher (controlling commercials and station breaks).

• **Personnel**

News director (ND) The news director, as the person with the top supervisory role and controlling interest in the newscast, is always peripherally involved in all stages of newscast production. Hence, the news director is

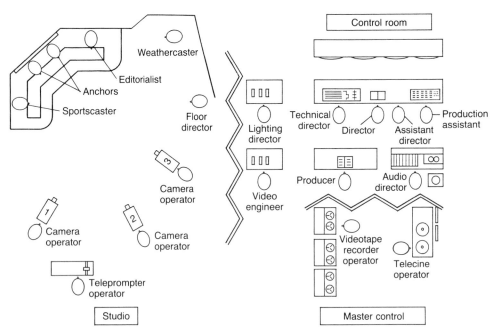

FIGURE 2–22
Newscast production personnel placement. This diagram indicates the placement of all newscast personnel during studio production.

expected to be close by during production, if only from the news director's office or from the newsroom itself.

News producer (P) The news producer is the production supervisor among all preproduction producers who remains present during studio production. Because the news producer is responsible for getting the news coverage and news producing tasks assigned at the newscast planning conference accomplished, the news producer is present in the control room to trouble-shoot any production problems and to clarify and explain any questions regarding elements of the newscast's format.

Talent (T) The talent is the center of the activity in the production. Talent includes anchor(s) or co-anchor(s), depending on the choice of roles given them; weathercaster; and sportscaster. Other talent could include special assignment producers or beat reporters.

Editorialist (E) The editorialist who serves as talent is listed separately for the following reasons: (1) if the editorialist is a staff member of the television station, writing and delivering the editorial is part of the job description of the role and not viewed strictly as talent, and (2) because not all newscasts use editorialists.

Studio director (D) During studio production, the studio director is the center of a wheel from whom all spokes radiate. Many see the studio director in television production as a conductor of an orchestra. Both analogies apply. The studio director is the center of and controls all of the individuals and activity that go into the production of a newscast. From the control room, with headset intercom connections to principal players, the studio director calls every change in video and audio signals.

Assistant director (AD) The assistant director plays a strong supporting role to the director during production. The assistant director has to know the format/rundown sheet; has a list of all prerecorded times of video stories and packages; and sets, activates, and reads the times of all stop watches, timers, and counters measuring the front time to the newscast, the back times, and all segment times. The assistant director also keeps track of character generator copy readied for matte into the program.

Technical director (TD) The technical director is the principal technician who assembles the newscast during production. The technical director responds to all the directorial calls of the studio director and effects each video change throughout the program. Because the newscast is a fully scripted production with a regular format/rundown, the technical director may anticipate a studio director's calls with the studio director's permission. This mutual working relationship develops over many newscasts, but the ability of the technical director to anticipate video changes can improve the pacing of the newscast.

Production assistant (PA) The production assistant is responsible to recall from the memory storage of the character generator any and all text copy entered from the character generator master list during preproduction.

Audio director (A) The audio director has the responsibility to channel the live in-studio or prerecorded audio sources designed by the news producer into the newscast.

Floor director (F) The floor director functions during studio production as the director's alter ego or second self. The floor director is the persona of the director in the studio, communicating and effecting the director's calls involving studio personnel, especially the talent. The floor director is responsible for communicating back to the director the situation in the studio and its personnel during production.

Camera operators (CO) The camera operators perform the most important role of providing the necessary studio-originated video. This means covering the talent during the presentation of the script.

Teleprompter operator (TO) The prompter operator has the responsibility to video and transmit the talent reading copy of the script via camera mounted monitors to the talent during the newscast.

Telecine operator (TC) The telecine operator operates from the master control area where the telecine is usually located. The telecine holds those 35mm and 16mm film sources that will be used in the newscast's production. The telecine operator either operates the telecine manually or routes control remotely to the assistant director in the control room.

Lighting director (LD) The lighting director is part of the studio production crew for purposes of monitoring the light levels on the set and talent and for changing the intensity of the lights should some dimming be part of the production values.

Videotape recorder operator (VTRO) The videotape recorder operator operates in the master control area of the television production facility. The primary role of the videotape recorder operator is to cue up and roll all videotape sources for A-roll and B-roll into the newscast and the record deck should the newscast be recorded as well as telecast.

Video engineer (VEG) The video engineer monitors the operation of all studio cameras during production. The video engineer adjusts lens aperture settings as light levels change during production. The video engineer also monitors soft focus from cameras and calls to the studio director to have camera operators adjust by fine focusing.

• **Production Stages**

Making a last minute check with the studio director and newscast talent (ND 1) The responsibility of the news director over the newscast extends to the production stage in addition to the preproduction and producing stages. The news director makes contact with the studio director and talent who represent the key players for the news director during production.

Making a last minute check with the studio director and newscast talent (NP 1) Similar to the role of the news director, the news producer also makes a final check with the studio director and the talent. The news producer is responsible for taking the assignments and directions from the newscast planning conference and getting the newscast produced. The news producer then becomes, in production, the best spokesperson to answer questions about the format/rundown sheet or to trouble-shoot last minute problems.

Monitoring the newscast production from a staff office or the newsroom (ND 2) The news director monitors the newscast production from a staff office or the newsroom. This permits the news director to keep an eye on the production without being intrusive or intimidating. Monitoring the newscast by the news director will result in its critique after the studio wrap.

Monitoring the newscast from the control room during the newscast production (NP 2) The news producer is a valuable resource to the format/rundown of the production and needs to be close to the production. The best place for the news producer to monitor the production is the control room in open communication with the studio director.

Communicating with the studio director on content and format problems and changes during the production (NP 3) The news producer's primary role during production is to be in communication with the studio director and the control room personnel. This permits ready questions on changes and format during production.

Monitoring all studio, control room, and master control set-ups and readiness before production begins (D 1) The studio director's primary responsibility in the early production stages is to monitor the readiness of all production crew. This means either asking over the intercom for state of readiness or receiving the ready call from crew members.

Assisting the studio director with preproduction details (AD 1) The assistant director remains at the side of the director and assists in any task that facilitates the beginning of production. The best assistance is knowledge of the format/rundown sheet, video sources listing, and character generator master list content.

Checking the format/rundown sheet for last minute updates (AD 2) The assistant director keeps abreast of all format/rundown sheet updates and informs the studio director of any changes.

Familiarizing self with format/rundown sheet and its updates (TD 1) Some of the news producer's last minute checks with control room crew may have involved updating the format/rundown sheet. When changes are made to the format/rundown sheet, the technical director has to be informed and thus be familiar with the updates.

Entering last minute data and other changes into the character generator (PA 1) The production assistant may also receive last minute additions and changes to the character generator copy. Existing data will have to be changed or updated.

Reviewing the format/rundown sheet for order and any changes in lighting needs (LD 1) The lighting director needs to know of any changes in the order of the newscast and those changes that affect lighting requirements.

Checking the lighting pattern on the set and the lighting instruments (LD 2) The lighting director checks

FIGURE 2–23
The lighting director. The lighting director monitors all stages of newscast lighting from the director's clocking to light intensity.

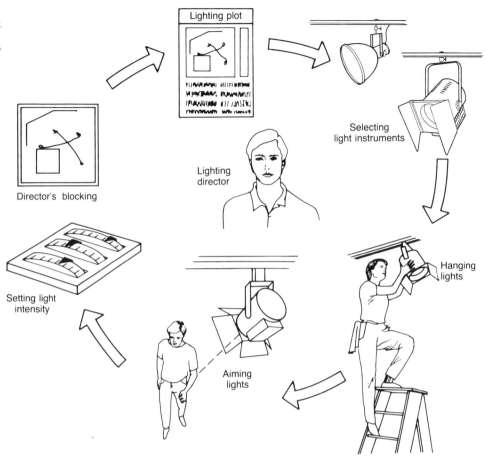

Lighting plot

Director's blocking

Lighting director

Selecting light instruments

Hanging lights

Setting light intensity

Aiming lights

the set for the lighting pattern designed on the lighting plot. Part of checking the set lighting includes checking for each assigned light instrument.

Checking lighting effects over studio camera monitors (LD 3) As part of checking overall set lighting, the lighting director needs to see how the whole set looks with the lights on over the control room monitors.

Checking for unwanted light reflection of the teleprompter monitors (LD 4) The lighting director checks the teleprompter monitors on each camera for unwanted light reflections and glare from studio lights. The reflections from studio lights and glare can create blind spots for the talent on the reading area of the monitor's screen These spots have to be corrected before production.

Making lighting intensity or light instrument changes (LD 5) The lighting director makes those changes that correct unwanted light glare and reflections by altering light intensity or re-aiming light instruments.

Alerting the director when lighting is ready (LD 6) The lighting director informs the studio director when the lighting is ready for production.

Readying the studio cameras for videotaping by shading (VEG 1) Once the lighting is set, the video engineer prepares the studio cameras for shading by lining them up together in front of the lighted set and locking them

down for shading. The cameras are then focused on the same lighted test area.

Checking video levels of the cameras with the lighting on the studio set (VEG 2) The video engineer checks the video light levels entering the camera lenses with the lighting intensity on the studio set. These are the light levels that the video engineer monitors throughout production.

Alerting the director when ready (VEG 3) The video engineer alerts the director when the cameras are ready.

Reviewing the format/rundown sheet for studio microphone needs, prerecorded audio sources, and playback audio needs and updates (A 1) The audio director keeps abreast of any additions or updates to the format/rundown sheet for the need for additional microphones, prerecorded audio sources, or playback audio feeds (e.g., from B-roll videotape) through the audio board for the production.

Reviewing the format/rundown sheet for studio expectations and order of updates (F 1) The floor director needs to be aware of changes and updates to the newscast as listed on the format/rundown sheet.

Reviewing the format/rundown sheet for camera needs, changes, updates (CO 1) The camera operators need to be apprised of changes and updates to their studio

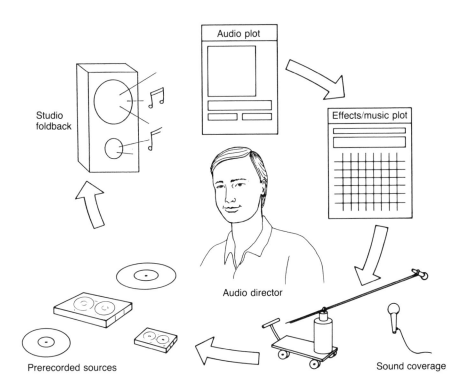

Audio plot

Studio foldback

Effects/music plot

Audio director

Prerecorded sources

Sound coverage

FIGURE 2–24
The audio director. The audio director monitors all phases of sound recording and coverage from the studio director's blocking on the audio plot to studio foldback.

performance needs as indicated on the format/rundown sheet.

Reviewing the format/rundown sheet for updates (TO 1) The teleprompter operator reviews the format/rundown sheet for updates or changes in the order of the newscast that affect the script prompting.

Reviewing the format/rundown sheet and graphics list for newscast order, changes, or updates (TC 1) Changes or updates on the format/rundown sheet may affect the order of film sources at the telecine. The telecine operator must become familiar with any changes on the format/rundown sheet.

Reviewing the format/rundown sheet for newscast order, changes, or updates (T 1) Talent checks the format/rundown sheet for any updates or changes that involve the talent's performance.

Reviewing the format/rundown sheet for newscast order, changes, or updates (E 1) The editorialist needs to be informed of any format/rundown changes that affect the performance of the editorialist. Any change of order within the newscast could affect the editorialist.

Reviewing the format/rundown sheet for videotape playback or record needs, changes, or updates (VTRO 1) Any format/rundown sheet updates involving the videotape playback or record needs or changes requires attention from the videotape recorder operator.

Securing talent copy (or copies) of the script (T 2) The talent must secure the script from the script editor. This is the first opportunity the talent has to see the script.

Securing the editorialist's copy of the script (E 2) The editorialist needs to secure the editorialist's copy of the script from the script editor. This is the first opportunity the editorialist has to see the editorial script since it was edited and approved.

Orienting to assigned video source monitors (D 2) The studio director takes time and orients to any new (as well as old) video source monitor assignments to the wall of monitors facing the studio director and the control room staff. Video sources assignment to videotape decks and control room monitors is the responsibility of the videotape recorder operator during preproduction. The technical director may already be alerted to the assignment of sources and can be of assistance to the studio director.

Orienting to all video source monitors (AD 3) The assistant director orients to all of the video source monitors facing the control room staff. The assistant director is a resource to the director during production by being a second check on video sources routing orientation to the control room.

Checking the intercom network connections and response stations (D 3) The studio director checks (or assigns) all intercom network connections important to the studio director during production. The best way to check on an intercom connection is to call each intercom station and exact a response from the production crew member.

Checking all intercom network connections (AD 4) The assistant director checks all of the intercom network connections that are important to the assistant director. The best check on the intercom connections is to ask for

```
PRESIDENT BUSH

TODAY ANNOUNCED

HIS NOMINEE TO

REPLACE RETIRING

SUPREME COURT

JUSTICE BRENNAN.

BUSH IS NOMINATING

DAVID H. SOUTER.

SOUTER IS A 50 YEAR

OLD APPEALS COURT

JUSTICE FROM NEW

HAMPSHIRE. BUSH IS
                    MORE
```

FIGURE 2–25
The newscast script. This is a sample of a newscast script. The text is arranged to the right side to be picked up by the studio prompter. The text is double spaced, which will allow for the insertion of interpretation marks. The left side of the page will allow the studio director to make notations.

a response from the crew members on the respective intercom stations.

Checking intercom network connections (TD 2) The technical director requires some intercom connections during the production, and each of these is individually checked for a working connection. The best check is to solicit a crew response. An important intercom connection for the technical director is with the videotape recorder operator.

Reviewing recorded character generator information with the assistant director (PA 2) The production assistant has the assistant director review all recorded data in the character generator. This ensures the production assistant of accuracy and informs the assistant director of character generator copy available.

Reviewing the character generator recorded copy (AD 5) The assistant director reviews all recorded character generator copy to check the production assistant for accuracy and to become familiar with the character generator copy available.

Keeping the character generator screen information current (PA 3) The production assistant keeps the character generator copy screen page current and ready for the next listed memory page.

Checking the studio microphone connections (A 2) The audio director, in a final studio run, checks the connections of all microphone cables. It is not uncommon with the presence of studio talent and production personnel that cables are pulled or caught and become detached.

Organizing the studio set for readiness and replacing props on spike marks (F 2) The floor director pays constant attention to changes on the studio set. With talent coming and going and the movement of the studio production crew, the set and props need reorganizing before production begins.

Checking intercom network connections (A 3) The audio director checks each of the intercom network connections important to the audio director. The best check is to receive a response from the production crew member on the network. Important intercom connections to the audio director are with the director and assistant director.

Checking the camera for zoom, pan, tilt, dolly, truck, pedestal, and arc control (CO 2) The camera operator takes the time at the camera before production to make a fast run through the main movements required of their cameras. These movements include the zoom, pan, tilt, dolly, truck, pedestal, and arc control.

Securing the teleprompter copy from the script editor (TO 2) The prompter operator secures the prompter copy of the production script from the script editor and prepares it for the teleprompter bed. The separate pages of the script may have to be taped together in order to facilitate its preparation for the prompter bed.

Securing adequate camera cable behind studio cameras for movement flexibility (CO 3) Each camera operator secures enough camera cable directly behind each camera to ensure enough flexible camera movement without cable drag on the camera during movement.

Loading the telecine with 35mm slides or 16mm film as necessary (TC 2) The telecine operator loads the telecine with whatever film sources, 35mm slides or 16mm film, are going to be used during production. The order of 35mm slides is indicated on the format/rundown sheet.

Checking intercom network connections at each camera (CO 4) The camera operators check their intercom network connections in order to be able to hear the studio director's calls during production. The best check is to get a response from the studio director. The camera operators need only a one way intercom connection during production—from the director to the camera operator.

Practicing required shots of the talent (CO 5) Camera operators take production preparation time to practice the defined shots of the talent that will be required during newscast production. Fast camera break movements should also be practiced.

Checking lens filter choice (CO 6) Camera operators make a final check that the correct filter has been chosen and is properly in place before the camera lens. This

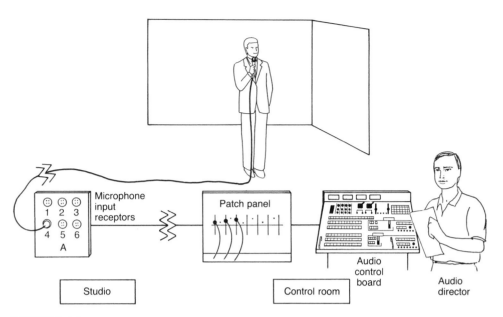

FIGURE 2–26
Studio microphone patching. Patching microphone cables with a sequence of connections is an important preproduction job for the audio director.

implies that a filter is required as a production value (e.g., a star filter for shooting studio lights). In some instances the visual effect will not be noticed clearly enough over the camera monitor, and camera operators will have to check with the video engineer, who has a more accurate reading of a filter in place.

Maintaining depth of field focus during and after changes in camera position (CO 7) Camera operators need practice and reminders to correct depth of field whenever the camera changes position during production. Camera operators must practice camera movements and rack focusing (the rapid zoom-in to refocus and zoom-out to reestablish the defined shot). Fine focusing without rack focusing should also be practiced (i.e., sensitive focus adjusting as talent or camera have to move).

Reading the script for familiarity with the copy and identifying pronunciation problems (T 3) The talent reads the script, checking that the typed copy reads with a style and grammatical familiarity. Talent checks that there are no pronunciation problems; if there are, correction and proper pronunciation are checked with the news producer.

Marking the teleprompter copy of the script for reading interpretation (T 4) The talent marks the teleprompter copy for reading interpretation (e.g., pauses and emphasis) and for the pronunciation of difficult or unfamiliar words. Talent should be aware that generally we are more visually literate (i.e., we recognize with the eye more vocabulary words than we really know how to pronounce) than audially (i.e., we may never have vocalized some words). This breeds a tendency to think that we can read all words properly. Talent should never guess at the pronunciation of words. Break into syllables (i.e.,

separate the word into its parts), phoneticize (i.e., rewrite the parts as monosyllabic sound-alike words where possible), and accentuate (i.e., graphically indicate the stressed syllable) all unfamiliar words on the space above the typed words on the prompter copy.

Reading the script for familiarity and pronunciation problems (E 3) The editorialist follows the same procedure as the talent: read the script for style and grammatical familiarity, and words for pronunciation problems. If any problem is discovered, the editorialist should check with the news producer.

Marking the teleprompter copy of the editorial for reading ease (E 4) When the editorialist discovers difficult words to pronounce, a check of the correct pronunciation should be made and the correct syllables, phonetic sounding of the syllables, and the proper accent should be written above the word on the teleprompter copy.

Preparing teleprompter copy for the teleprompter bed (TO 3) The prompter operator takes the copy of the talent marked script and places it on the teleprompter bed. Under the teleprompter video camera, the script is reproduced over the monitors on the front of the studio cameras. The copy has to be attached to some form of tractor feed and the video pick-up camera has to be aimed and focused as part of the teleprompter bed preparation.

Checking the video reproduction of the script from the teleprompter bed to the camera monitors (TO 4) The teleprompter operator makes a check that the teleprompter script reproduces acceptably on the monitors on the front of the studio cameras. In some cases, the camera monitor requires adjustment for contrast and brightness.

PRESIDENT BUSH

TODAY ANNOUNCED
NAH-MEN-KNEE
HIS NOMINEE TO

REPLACE RETIRING

SUPREME COURT

JUSTICE BRENNAN. //

BUSH IS NOMINATING
SUIT-ER
DAVID H. SOUTER. //
UH
SOUTER IS A 50 YEAR

OLD APPEALS COURT

JUSTICE FROM NEW
HAM-SURE
MORE   HAMPSHIRE. /BUSH SAYS

FIGURE 2–27
Marking interpretation notes on the prompter script copy. Newscast talent should make pronunciation, emphasis, pauses, and other meaningful notations that will assist correct reading of the copy.

Permitting talent to check reading pleasure and practice with the script and checking the foldback sound in the studio (TO 5)   The teleprompter operator takes the opportunity to permit the talent to check both the reading height of the text on the teleprompter screen and the speed of the script. During this practice, the prompter operator checks the volume level of studio foldback so the talent voice can be heard adequately for the prompter operator to be able to follow with the script.

Setting levels for playback audio cartridge sources (A 4)   The audio director needs to play back each audio cartridge source to set gain, equalization, and tone levels for each source. The audio sources must then be re-cued to first audio starting point.

Getting dressed and applying make-up (T 5)   After the talent reviews the script and marks it for reading, the talent retires to a dressing room to get dressed with on-air wardrobe and to put on make-up.

Getting dressed and applying make-up (E 5)   The editorialist retires to a dressing room and dresses for the newscast and applies make-up.

Checking and re-cuing all prerecorded audio sources (A 5)   The audio director takes the time to check and then re-cue all prerecorded audio sources controlled from the audio booth.

Reporting to the set and maintaining spike marks (T 6)   The talent reports to the floor director and the studio set as soon as the talent is dressed and made-up for the newscast. Spike marks on the set are part of the newscast design and are used for staging consistency. The talent must maintain the spike marks while working on the set.

Reporting to the studio set (E 6)   Once the editorialist dresses and puts on make-up, the editorialist reports to the floor director and awaits the time at which the editorialist is to enter the set. Once on the set, the editorialist must hit and maintain spike marks.

Patching and testing foldback sound to the studio (A 6)   The audio director patches the foldback sound to the studio. The foldback sound will allow the studio crew to hear the audio program line from the audio booth. This permits the studio crew to keep tabs on audio out-cues during production. The foldback sound is tested for gain level to avoid feedback. The teleprompter operator also relies on foldback to follow the talent reading voice.

Calling for studio talent microphone checks and setting levels for each (A 7)   With foldback in working order, the audio director now calls into the studio for talent microphone checks. This entails asking the talent to use the microphone naturally and read some copy into it until the audio director sets gain, equalization, and tone levels for each talent microphone.

Performing microphone checks at the request of the audio director (T 7)   The audio director calls a microphone level check into the studio and requests that all talent, one at a time, offer some vocalization over the microphone. This requires that each talent speak in a normal tone of voice (i.e., the tone to be used on the air) into the microphone. A normal response is to begin counting until the audio director signals completion of the microphone test. Counting consecutively is a good test because talent can continue until the test is finished. Often talent offer too little text for the audio director to be able to test the microphone and set levels adequately. This necessitates the audio director calling again into the studio for more testing and vocalization. During the microphone test, talent microphones should be in place (e.g., pinned onto a suit) and not lifted to the mouth.

Checking teleprompter monitors for reading ease and light reflections (T 8)   The talent takes the opportunity to practice reading the teleprompter for reading ease as well as checking for annoying light reflections or glare from the teleprompter monitor screens.

Checking teleprompter monitors for reading ease (E 7)   The editorialist should check the teleprompter monitors for ease in reading. This includes a check for prompter operating speed as well as light glare or reflections from monitor screens.

Having the floor director check make-up and making repairs (T 9)   Before giving a ready signal, the talent should have the floor director check make-up for perspiration shine and have the make-up repaired by powdering.

Having the floor director check make-up and making repairs (E 8)   The editorialist has the floor director check make-up for perspiration shine and make powdering repairs to the make-up.

Alerting the floor director when ready (T 10)   The talent alerts the floor director when the talent is ready to begin production.

Alerting the floor director when ready (E 9) The editorialist alerts the floor director when the editorialist is ready for production.

Alerting the floor director when ready (TO 6) The teleprompter operator informs the floor director when the script and the prompter bed are ready.

Resetting the countdown timer(s) and checking the stop watch(es) or counters for front, back, and segment times during production (AD 6) The assistant director sets all timing devices in the control room to measure the front time (i.e., from 00:00 to 28:30), back time (i.e., from 28:30 to 00:00), and segment times (i.e., the individual times of preproduced video stories and packages) of the newscast.

Choosing playback and record videotape recorders to handle A-roll and B-roll video requirements for the newscast production and alerting the technical director of the choices made for signal routing purposes (VTRO 2) From the videotape recorder operator's analysis of the format/rundown sheet and the master videotapes supplied by the news producer, the videotape recorder operator evaluates the playback decks required for the newscast and the requirement of a record deck. With the customary need for B-rolling videotape into a news program, at the minimum, two alternating playback decks may be required. Even in a live telecast, there is often the need to make a videotape recording of the program. When choices are made of videotape recorders,

the videotape recorder operator informs the technical director of the choices for signal routing of the video from the decks through the production switcher as well as for the assignment of studio monitors. The studio director and the assistant director are also interested in the assignment of video signals to the control room before production.

Checking video playback routing through the switcher (TD 3) The technical director checks every video source signal routed through the switcher by striking the assigned buttons on the switcher and having the assistant director (if the playback decks are operated remotely) or videotape recorder operator (if the playback decks are operated manually) roll each deck and visually check the response.

Checking on the talent and monitoring their readiness (F 3) The floor director keeps a constant check on the talent, including the stages of necessary checks from microphone setting, marking script copy, hitting spike marks, and make-up. The floor director monitors talent readiness until production starting time.

Checking intercom network connections (F 4) The floor director checks all intercom network connections needed by the floor director to be in communication with the control room.

Checking on camera operators and monitoring their readiness (F 5) As the studio director's second self in

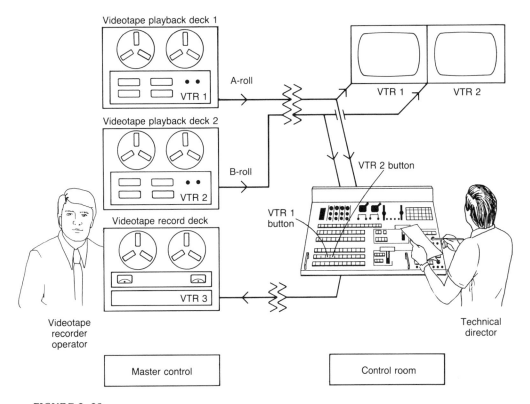

FIGURE 2–28
Assigning and routing A-roll and B-roll video sources. The videotape recorder operator has to determine and assign both A-roll and B-roll playback and record videotape decks for routing to the control room and to the production switcher.

the studio, the floor director constantly checks on the readiness of the camera operators before production begins. This includes camera operators' absence from the studio for restroom purposes.

Checking on lighting, light instruments, and lighting pattern working order (F 6) The floor director is constantly aware of studio details before and during production. One area of detail checking is all phases of studio lighting. Light bulbs can go out at any moment. Awareness of the lighting pattern on the set and aimed instruments are a part of the floor director's attention to studio details.

Checking the telecine for proper operation and the correct order of film sources (TC 3) The telecine operator makes a final check on the operation of the telecine—manual operation (if the telecine operator will advance the film sources during production) and remote operation (if the assistant director will advance the film sources). A final check is made of the order of film sources, especially the graphics, in the telecine.

Checking intercom network connections (TC 4) The telecine operator needs intercom connections with the studio director and the assistant director and these connections should be checked.

Checking audio foldback in the studio (F 7) The floor director keeps a constant check before production for the proper operation and gain level of the foldback sound in the studio.

Checking the video levels of videotape playback sources with the videotape recorder operator (TD 4) While rolling all videotape playback sources to check routing, the technical director checks the video levels of each video story or package. Video levels are checked through vectorscopes at the switcher. If levels are not acceptable, the videotape recorder operator makes adjustments in master control until video level readings are acceptable to the technical director.

Setting video levels of video playback sources with the technical director (VTRO 3) The videotape recorder operator responds to the technical director as each video source is checked by running the video until the technical director affirms acceptable video levels of each B-roll video through the switcher. The videotape recorder operator adjusts the video levels on each playback deck while the technical director reads the acceptable levels from the vectorscope at the switcher.

Setting audio levels for each playback video source (A 8) While the technical director and videotape recorder operator are checking each B-roll video story or package playback for video levels, the audio director takes the opportunity of the video playback to set audio levels for each video story or package. Setting audio levels involves recording the gain, equalization, and tone settings for each video. These settings will have to be recorded where they can be retrieved so they can be preset again before each video source plays.

Setting video clip levels at the switcher for video mattes (TD 5) The technical director checks the switcher clip level for all video matte sources to be used during production. Primary matte video sources are the character generator and the telecine. The technical director calls for a sample of each of these sources and sets its clip level.

Cuing up playback videotape decks for A-roll and B-roll videotape (VTRO 4) The videotape recorder operator cues up videotapes on the playback videotape decks to be used for A- and B-rolling videotape.

Threading the record videotape deck for record dub of the newscast (VTRO 5) The videotape recorder operator threads the record videotape deck in preparation for recording the newscast.

Switching the remote control of playback videotape decks to the control room and the assistant director (VTRO 6) The videotape recorder operator switches the remote control of playback videotape decks to the control room and the assistant director if this is required.

Alerting the studio director when ready (VTRO 7) The videotape recorder operator lets the studio director know when all elements of master control are ready for production.

Presetting any mix or effects buses for special effects (TD 6) The technical director presets the beginning special effects required for the newscast's opening. This usually takes some preset combination mix or effects buses.

Checking and presetting other special effects equipment available to the production (TD 7) The technical director will have to check and preset any other special effects sources to be used (e.g., still store memory access or squeeze zoom or video flip).

Making make-up checks on the talent and repairing when necessary (F 8) The floor director keeps a constant visual check on the make-up of the talent. Pressure and waiting can cause talent perspiration and facial oils to overpower make-up, which results in facial shining. The floor director repairs talent make-up with powder when necessary.

Awaiting a "ready" cue from production personnel: audio director, camera operators, lighting director, production assistant, technical director, floor director, talent, video engineer, and videotape recorder operator (D 4) The studio director comes to a moment in production preparation when production crew and talent have to indicate their readiness to begin. It is better if the director does not have to page all crew to check on their readiness. The crew members themselves should alert the director when they are ready.

Setting opening shots and alerting the floor director of readiness (CO 8) Camera operators indicate their readiness by setting their respective opening shots on their cameras and by alerting the studio director.

Alerting the studio director when ready (A 9) When all audio production checks have been made, the audio director signals the director that all audio sources are ready.

Alerting the studio director when the studio is ready (F 9) The floor director is the best positioned crew member to indicate to the studio director and the control room the state of readiness of the crew and talent.

Alerting the studio director when ready (TD 8) The technical director alerts the studio director when all checks and presets and the technical director are ready to begin.

Alerting the studio director when ready (PA 4) The production assistant lets the studio director know when the character generator copy is recorded, stored in memory, checked for accuracy, and ready.

Communicating readiness to the assistant director (TC 5) The telecine operator lets the assistant director know when the telecine and film sources are ready for production.

Calling a stand-by cue to all studio, control room, and master control crew members (D 5) The studio director cues the production crew by calling a stand-by as a signal that production is about to begin. This alerts all crew—in the studio, control room, and master control area.

Preparing to follow the script for the director (AD 7) The assistant director prepares to follow the director's script as a stand-by call is announced. This generally means that the assistant director uses a finger or pencil to point to the area of the script where the production is at any moment.

Communicating the studio director's commands to the studio personnel (F 10) The floor director relays all of the studio director's commands to the studio personnel aloud before production begins and by hand signals after production has begun.

Calling and maintaining readiness in the studio (F 11) The floor director relays the stand-by cue to the studio personnel and maintains crew attention and readiness until the director advances to the program opening.

Standing by with the floor director's call (T 11) The talent takes a stand-by position as the floor director relays the studio director's call for a stand-by.

Attending to the floor director for the opening cue to begin (TO 7) The prompter operator pays attention to the floor director for the cue from the director to begin running the teleprompter script for the talent.

Listening for the studio director's call for lighting cues and changes (LD 7) The lighting director listens for any cues from the studio director to begin or to make any lighting changes. A production value of the newscast may involve bringing the lights up on cue or down on cue.

Calling to the videotape recorder operator a "ready to roll tape" and to cue to "roll videotape" (D 6) When the studio director is ready to begin production or real clock time for telecast has arrived, the studio director cues the beginning of videotape recording by calling for a "ready to roll videotape." The studio director awaits the videotape recorder operator's response that the tape is ready. The studio director then calls for the videotape to begin rolling.

Responding to the studio director's call to ready the videotape deck and to roll the videotape by readying the videotape deck and then beginning to operate it (VTRO 8) The videotape recorder operator stands by by readying the videotape deck and by rolling the videotape—actually operating the deck—when the director calls to ready the videotape deck and then to roll the videotape.

Awaiting real clock time and counting down the final seconds to the newscast opening (D 7) The studio director watches the real clock time for telecast start time and counts down the remaining seconds to the start. If the newscast is not being telecast live, the production starting time is at the discretion of the director.

Awaiting the studio director's opening cues (A 10) The audio director awaits the studio director's opening cues that may involve audio control sources.

Reading loudly the clock and timer countdowns and other time cues during production (AD 8) The assistant director watches all clocks and timers and reads 10-second (:10) countdown times loudly for all in the control room and those over the intercom to hear. The assistant director begins this service for the opening of the newscast and continues throughout the production for all beginning cues to the closing time for the newscast.

Repeating all 10-second (:10) countdowns to the studio to a 2-second (:02) call (F 12) The floor director repeats all of the studio director's (or assistant director's) 10-second countdowns to the studio by counting aloud down to the 2-second count. The remaining seconds are counted silently by all studio production crew so that unwanted sounds are not picked up by the microphones.

Signaling to the talent which cameras are "on" (F 13) The floor director signals to the talent whenever a camera change is made by the studio director by indicating which camera to change to and which camera is then "on." These signals are hand signals during videotaping.

Beginning with the floor director's signal from the studio director to begin and noting when the camera tally light goes on (T 12) The talent begins to read the script when the floor director signals the studio director's cue to begin. Affirming that signal to begin is the tally light operation on the opening camera.

Directing the script, reading the preproduction notations and cues on the script, readying audio and video sources, and taking all formatted sources (D 8) Having begun the newscast, the studio director follows the script with the assistance of the assistant director. The studio director now uses those notations and cues written on the script during preproduction. All video and audio sources indicated on the format/rundown sheet are readied and taken by the director when noted in the script.

Listening to, readying for, and responding to the director's commands (TD 9) The technical director listens carefully to all of the studio director's commands during newscast production, readies the command, and prepares to respond with the appropriate video source change.

Switching appropriate video sources (TD 10) The technical director faithfully responds to all of the studio director's commands to the technical director by appropriately changing the video sources through the switcher.

Following the studio director's calls during production (A 11) The audio director follows all cues referring to audio sources into the newscast.

Maintaining communication between the studio director and the studio (F 14) The floor director maintains two-way communication between the studio director and the production crew.

Maintaining ready positions until the studio director calls for a new set-up (CO 9) Camera operators keep their defined and readied camera shots (i.e., framing) in position until the studio director calls for a new camera shot set-up.

Advancing the character generator screen copy when the technical director clears the previous matte from the program line (PA 5) The production assistant advances the character generator screen copy as previous pages are used and matted into the newscast program. The production assistant can properly change and preview succeeding copy only when the technical director has removed any previous matte copy from the program line. This procedure is used unless character generator copy must change on screen while on the program line.

Following the talent carefully and keeping the script copy at the desired screen height (TO 8) The teleprompter operator follows the talent script reading very carefully over studio foldback and keeps the script copy at the desired screen height for each talent.

Reading loudly expected out-cues to all video stories and packages (AD 9) The assistant director loudly reads expected out-cues to all video stories and packages as they B-roll into the newscast. Out-cues are the final few words of copy or visual images at the end of a prerecorded video news story or package. Knowing the expected out-cues permits crew members to anticipate the end of the video and effect changes in the program. Video producers provide out-cues on their edited master clipsheets, the

studio director notes those cues on the script, and the assistant director reads those cues from the director's script during production.

Keeping close tabs on all timed prerecorded video sources (AD 10) During the B-roll of all prerecorded video sources, the assistant director keeps accurate time with a stop watch. The times of all prerecorded video sources—times usually from first audio (or first video) to final audio (or final video)—are reported by feature producers on the edited master clipsheets. The studio director transfers these times to the script; the assistant director reads the times from the studio director's script and times the B-roll video as it is inserted into the program.

Operating and advancing or monitoring the telecine during production (TC 6) The telecine operator either operates and advances the film sources at the telecine throughout the newscast or monitors the telecine as the assistant director operates and advances the film sources by remote control from the control room.

Operating and advancing the telecine as needed or communicating the cue to operate and advance the telecine (AD 11) The assistant director either operates and advances telecine film sources by remote control or communicates the cues to operate and advance the telecine to the telecine operator during production.

Operating videotape playback decks by remote control or readying the videotape playback sources for operation (AD 12) The assistant director operates the videotape playback decks if they are controlled from the control room by remote control. If the videotape recorder operator operates the playback decks manually, the assistant director readies the videotape playback sources for operation. A pre-roll time of 3 to 5 seconds is anticipated in some production operations.

Readying all character generator screen copy (AD 13) The assistant director readies all character generator screen copy for insertion into the newscast. Notation for character generator copy insert is among the notations and cues the studio director added to the script during preproduction.

Alerting the studio director and the assistant director to unused character generator copy (PA 6) The production assistant alerts the studio director and the assistant director if any preplanned character generator copy has gone unnoticed or unused.

Communicating to the talent during commercial breaks any changes from the studio director or the news producer (F 15) The floor director takes the opportunity of commercial breaks to communicate to the talent any changes or messages from the studio director or the news producer.

Repairing talent make-up during commercial breaks (F 16) The floor director takes commercial break time to check and powder the talent's make-up to diminish any shine.

Communicating to the studio director any information from the studio or studio crew (F 17) The floor director communicates using two-way communication with the studio director to relay any information (e.g., questions) from the studio crew to the studio director.

Listening to and following the studio director's calls during production (CO 10) Camera operators listen carefully and follow all of the studio director's calls regarding their cameras.

Standing by for any changes or corrections from the telecine film sources during the newscast and reloading sources if necessary (TC 7) The telecine operator, whether operating the telecine manually or monitoring its remote control operation, stands by for any changes or corrections needed from the telecine film sources during production. When 35mm slides are being used in production, the necessity to have to reload the telecine's slide drums is always a possibility.

Following the floor director's communication (T 13) The talent prepares to follow any communication from the floor director, whether the commands are given verbally during commercial breaks or by hand signals during production.

Repairing or having repairs to make-up during commercial breaks (T 14) The stress of on-air demands as well as the heat generated from studio lighting will cause talent make-up to need constant repair. The talent may choose to repair the talent's own make-up by powdering or may allow the floor director to assist. It is the floor director who keeps a constant vigil on the need for talent make-up repair. Powdering repairs to make-up are made during commercial breaks.

Monitoring playback and record videotape decks (VTRO 9) The videotape recorder operator constantly monitors all videotape recording decks during production. The videotape recorder operator monitors the decks by reading the audio and video output levels on the decks.

Monitoring the video light levels of cameras (VEG 4) The video engineer monitors the video light levels of all cameras during production. When light levels and talent change, lens apertures have to be changed accordingly.

Alerting the studio director to any soft focused cameras during production (VEG 5) The video engineer monitors the cameras' video output for any soft focused cameras and alerts the studio director to pass the information along to the offending camera operator for fine focusing.

Standing by for the floor director's call to begin (E 10) The editorialist stands by until alerted by the floor director for the instruction to take an assigned place on the set and to await the cue to begin.

Beginning the editorial with the floor director's signal from the studio director and tally light operation (E 11) The editorialist begins the delivery of the editorial at the floor director's signal from the studio director. That

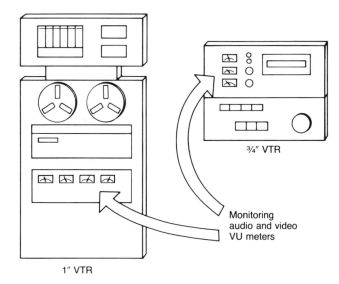

¾" VTR

Monitoring audio and video VU meters

1" VTR

FIGURE 2–29
Monitoring audio and video VU meters. The videotape recorder operator has to monitor the audio and video signal VU meters on videotape decks to ensure a constant signal during production. Lost or missing signals can mean a delay in production.

signal is confirmed when the tally light on the camera goes on.

Following the floor director's communications (E 12) As for any studio talent, the editorialist follows all of the floor director's communications to the editorialist.

Conferring with the news producer for any content or format decisions (D 9) The studio director defers to the news producer during production for any questions that arise regarding the newscast's content or format.

Making content decisions with final timing of the newscast (NP 4) The news producer evaluates the time remaining in the newscast and makes any necessary content decisions (e.g., to delete some content if the newscast is running long or to add some pad content if the newscast is running short) and conveys those decisions to the studio director.

Closing the newscast (D 10) The studio director brings the newscast production to a close following real clock time or newscast front or back time.

Announcing any postproduction needs (D 11) The studio director decides with the counsel of the news producer whether to make any postproduction changes or corrections to the recording. This would be a consideration only if the newscast were a tape-delayed telecast or if postproduction is even possible and necessary. The studio director announces a decision on postproduction needs to the production crew or calls a studio wrap.

Preparing for any postproduction needs from subordinate crew or helping complete the studio wrap (AD 14) The assistant director reacts to the studio director's call for postproduction by activating subordinate crew to respond or assists in the call for a studio wrap.

Preparing for any postproduction or stopping down the switcher at the studio director's call for a wrap (TD 11) The technical director either prepares to continue in the technical director's role in postproduction or stops down the switcher at the studio director's call for a wrap.

Preparing for any postproduction or turning off the character generator at the call for a wrap (PA 7) The production assistant either prepares to continue character generator control during postproduction or turns the character generator off at the call for a wrap.

Preparing for any postproduction needs or striking the audio set-up at the call for a wrap (A 12) The audio director either prepares to contribute audio production elements if needed in postproduction or strikes the audio set-up at the call for a wrap.

Relaying the studio director's call for a hold in studio positions pending a call for postproduction or for a studio wrap (F 18) The floor director relays the studio director's call to hold studio positions pending a decision to do postproduction involving the studio crew or the announcement that the production is complete and the call is to strike the set at the studio director's wrap call.

Holding studio positions pending a decision to do postproduction work or striking the cameras at a studio wrap (CO 11) Camera operators either hold their positions pending the studio director's decision to do some postproduction that may involve the studio cameras or they begin to strike the cameras at the studio director's call for a wrap.

Holding prompter position pending the studio director's decision to do studio postproduction work involving the script or beginning to strike the teleprompter at the call for a wrap (TO 9) The teleprompter operator either holds the studio position pending the director's decision to do some postproduction that involves the script or begins to strike the teleprompter equipment at the call for a wrap.

Holding the telecine operation pending the studio director's decision to do postproduction or beginning to strike the telecine and film sources at the call for a wrap (TC 8) The telecine operator either holds at the telecine awaiting the studio director's decision to do postproduction that might involve the film sources or prepares to strike the telecine and film sources.

Holding studio position(s) pending the director's decision to do postproduction involving the talent or preparing for a studio wrap (T 15) The talent holds the position at the floor director's command pending the studio director's decision to do postproduction involving the talent or prepares for the studio wrap by cleaning the anchor desk area at the wrap call.

Preparing for any postproduction involving lighting or beginning to strike set lighting at the studio director's call for a wrap (LD 8) The lighting director prepares to contribute to postproduction if lighting needs are involved or begins to strike set lighting with the call for a wrap.

Preparing for any videotape recording postproduction needs for which the studio director may call or beginning to strike the videotape and shut down the videotape decks (VTRO 10) The videotape recorder operator will be involved in any postproduction on the newscast. The videotape recorder operator awaits the director's call. At a studio wrap, the videotape recorder operator begins to shut down the videotape decks.

Preparing for postproduction needs for which the studio director may call involving studio cameras or beginning to strike the cameras by capping the lenses (VEG 6) The video engineer prepares for the studio director's call to do postproduction involving the studio cameras or begins to strike the cameras and the video control area by capping the lenses of the cameras both electronically and physically.

Calling for a studio wrap (D 12) When the studio director feels that the production is finished, a studio wrap is called. A *wrap* means that the studio, control room, and master control personnel can strike equipment, videotape(s), and set, and the talent can leave the studio and remove make-up.

Rewinding videotapes at a studio wrap and labeling all videotapes and their storage cases (VTRO 11) The videotape recorder operator strikes the videotape decks by rewinding all videotape source tapes and the master videotape, labeling the videotapes and their storage cases.

THE POSTPRODUCTION PROCESS

If the newscast production just completed was telecast live, there is little reason to consider postproduction work on the newscast.

However, if the newscast is a tape-delayed telecast, some postproduction may be done. The individuals who have the authority to order postproduction work are the news director, the news producer, or the studio director.

• Personnel

There are only three personnel who have new roles in postproduction: the news director, the news producer, and the studio director.

News director (ND) Having monitored the newscast's production from an office or the newsroom, the news director may step into the studio production process by requiring some postproduction on the completed program. Because the news director is totally responsible for the newscast, the news director can decide if and what will be added or redone during postproduction.

News producer (NP) The news producer may take some responsibility for any problems or errors in the program. Problems and errors could be a fault at the producing stage of the production. Because the news producer is responsible for getting all assigned producing work done, the news producer can use that authority to require postproduction work on the program.

Studio director (D) The studio director may take responsibility for problems or mistakes that were created by the production crew under the studio director's supervision. The director can decide to do postproduction work on the program.

All other production crew members All remaining production crew members are the same as those defined at the production stage of the newscast. Roles and responsibilities remain identical to those performed during production.

• **Postproduction Stages**

Assuming some authority, responsibility, and a decision-making role in adding or redoing elements of the newscast (ND 1) The news director, from the newscast viewing vantage of an office or the newsroom during production, will take the authority and responsibility as well as a decision-making role in calling for the studio director to redo or add elements to the newscast in postproduction.

Communicating those elements of either the producing stage or the production stage of the newscast that will become part of the postproduction process (ND 2) The news director communicates to the studio director those elements of either the producing stage or the production stage of the newscast that are to become part of the postproduction process.

Continuing as in the production stage of the newscast (ND 3) The news director takes the same role as was the news director's role during the production stage.

Assuming a decision-making role to add or redo those elements of the newscast that involve producing errors or problems (NP 1) The news producer may decide that some elements of the newscast involved errors or problems in producing. The news producer takes responsibility for producing errors or problems and has the studio director begin postproduction with the appropriate production crew members involved in correcting and redoing portions of the newscast.

Communicating those elements of the producing stage of the newscast that will become a part of the postproduction process (NP 2) The news producer tells the director which parts of the newscast are producing errors or problems and will become part of the required postproduction.

Continuing as in the production stage (NP 3) The news producer continues during postproduction in the role as defined for the news producer in the production process.

Assuming authority, responsibility, and a decision-making role to add or redo elements of the newscast that involve studio production errors or problems and communicating these to the news director and news producer (D 1) The studio director may take the authority, responsibility, and decision-making role to correct and redo elements of the newscast that involve studio production errors or problems. The studio director communicates these intentions to the news director and the news producer.

Alerting the production crew members who will be involved in postproduction (D 2) The studio director informs those production crew members who will be involved in postproduction. For example, if postproduction involves only control room personnel, then studio personnel are given a wrap call.

Continuing as in the production stage (D 3) The studio director continues postproduction in the role the studio director had in the production stage.

Readying those crew members who will be involved in postproduction (AD 1) The assistant director readies those production crew members who will be involved in postproduction.

Continuing as in the production stage (AD 2) The assistant director continues in the role defined for the assistant director at the production stage.

Preparing to add or redo those elements of the newscast in postproduction that involve the production switcher (TD 1) The technical director prepares to add or redo those elements of the newscast in postproduction that involve the production switcher.

Communicating to the videotape recorder operator what video sources will be involved in postproduction (TD 2) The technical director communicates to the videotape recorder operator those video sources, if any, that will be involved in postproduction.

Continuing as in the production stage (TD 3) The technical director continues in the role defined for the technical director at the production stage.

Preparing to ready those elements of the character generator that will be involved in postproduction (PA 1) The production assistant prepares to ready any character generator copy that will be involved in the postproduction of the newscast.

Continuing as in the production stage (PA 2) The production assistant continues in the role defined for the production assistant at the production stage.

Preparing to ready those audio sources that will be involved in postproduction (A 1) The audio director prepares to ready any audio sources for which the audio director will be responsible during postproduction.

Continuing as in the production stage (A 2) The audio director continues in the role defined for the audio director at the production stage.

Preparing to ready and maintain control of those elements in the studio that will be involved in postproduction (F 1) The floor director has to keep studio personnel informed, get them ready, and maintain readiness for whatever elements, if any, involve the studio personnel in postproduction.

Continuing as in the production stage (F 2) The floor director assumes the role defined for the floor director at the production stage.

Preparing to ready those elements of the studio cameras that will be involved in postproduction (CO 1) The camera operators prepare to ready themselves and their cameras for whatever, if any, elements of the studio cameras may involve them in postproduction.

Continuing as in the production stage (CO 2) The camera operators continue in the role defined for them at the production stage.

Preparing to ready the teleprompter script for postproduction (TO 1) The teleprompter operator prepares to ready the script for use in postproduction if it is necessary.

Continuing as in the production stage (TO 2) The teleprompter operator continues in the role defined for the teleprompter operator and the script during the production stage.

Preparing to ready the film sources in the telecine for postproduction (TC 1) The telecine operator prepares to ready whatever film sources at the telecine may be required in postproduction.

Continuing as in the production stage (TC 2) The telecine operator continues in the role defined for the telecine operator at the production stage.

Preparing to redo any studio video and script copy for postproduction (T 1) The talent prepares to redo any studio video or script copy if it is required in postproduction.

Continuing as in the production stage of the newscast (T 2) The talent continues in the role defined for the studio talent at the production stage.

Preparing for redoing the editorial in postproduction (E 1) If the editorial needs to be redone as part of the postproduction, the editorialist prepares to deliver the script copy.

Continuing as in the production stage (E 2) The editorialist continues in the role defined for the editorialist at the production stage.

Readying those studio lighting elements that may be involved in postproduction (LD 1) The lighting director readies those studio lighting elements that may be involved in postproduction.

Continuing as in the production stage of the newscast (LD 2) The lighting director continues in the role defined for the lighting director at the production stage.

Readying the videotape decks for postproduction (VTRO 1) The videotape recorder operator readies the necessary videotape decks, playback and record, that may be involved in postproduction. At the least, the videotape recorder operator will have to cue up the record deck and oversee the recording of postproduction elements.

Continuing as in the production stage (VTRO 2) The videotape recorder operator continues during postproduction at the role defined for the videotape recorder operator in the production stage.

Readying the cameras and video levels for postproduction (VEG 1) The video engineer readies the cameras and their video levels if the studio cameras are involved in postproduction.

Continuing as in the production stage (VEG 2) The video engineer continues as at the production stage.

Chapter 3

Studio Production Organizing Forms

There is a diversity and breadth of roles and task responsibilities in television newscast producing and production unknown in other television genres. This very diversity and breadth warrant some technique within which role and task responsibility of personnel can be successfully met. It is frequently said in television production that the success of a production is a function of the extent and degree of preproduction.

Organizing forms are presented in this chapter for almost all information gathering and task preparation stages required for newscast preproduction and production. The majority of the forms serve to design and order newscast producing tasks. The remaining forms help to prepare for the actual studio production of the newscast. Included are forms that were designed to assist in the origination and design of a new newscast production. As with many resources in a creative and technological medium, not all forms will be equally functional. These forms should be used when they facilitate the tasks for which they were created. They should not become ends in themselves. Forms that serve the production should be used and perhaps adapted to the requirements of a particular newscast or news organization. Others may be needed and may serve a one time only function. Still others may not be required and should be overlooked.

The forms presented here are designed to be used by producing and production personnel for particular role accomplishment. Those roles are listed in the upper portions of the respective forms. These forms can be removed or photocopied. Note that each form's structure and function are detailed in Chapter 4.

PRODUCTION BUDGET

MULTIPLE CAMERA VIDEO NEWS PRODUCTION

News Director:

Executive Producer:

Date: / /

Preproduction Time per Newscast: Hours: ☐

No. Studio Production Days: ☐ Hours: ☐

Postproduction Time per Newscast: Hours: ☐

Newscast:

Newscast Length: :

Frequency: ☐daily ☐weekly ☐other

Newscast Production Period:

/ / to / /

No. of Newscasts: ☐

SUMMARY OF PRODUCTION COSTS	ESTIMATED	ACTUAL
1. Rights and Clearances		
2. Producing Staff and Expenses		
3. Director, Staff, and Expenses		
4. Talent		
5. Benefits		
6. Production Facility		
7. Production Staff		
8. Cameras, Videotape Recording, Video Engineering		
9. News Gathering Sources, Materials		
10. ENG News Gathering Costs		
11. News Set Design, Construction, Decoration, Props		
12. Set Lighting		
13. Audio Production		
14. Wardrobe, Make-up, Hairdressing		
15. Videotape Stock, Film Stock, Film Processing		
16. Postproduction Editing		
17. Music		
18.		
19. Subtotal		
20. Contingency		
Grand Total		

COMMENTS

RIGHTS AND CLEARANCES	ESTIMATED	ACTUAL
1. Rights Purchased		
2. Other Rights		
3. Title and Logo Trademark Registration		
4. Music Clearances		
5. Video Clearances		
6. Audio Clearances		
7. Other Clearances		
8.		
Subtotal		

PRODUCING STAFF

CREW	ESTIMATED				ACTUAL			
	Days	Rate	O/T Hrs	Total	Days	Rate	O/T Hrs	Total
9. News Director								
10. Preproduction								
11. Production								
12. Executive Producer								
13. Preproduction								
14. Production								
15. Assignment Editor								
16. Preproduction								
17. Production								
18. News Producer								
19. Preproduction								
20. Production								
21. Postproduction								
22. Secretary No. ( )								
23. Reporter/Writer								
24. Preproduction								
25. Production								
26. Feature Producer								
27. Preproduction								
28. Production								
29. Postproduction								
30. Script Editor								
31. Producing Supplies								
32. Photocopying								
33. Telephone								
34. Postage								
35. Travel Expenses								
36. Per Diem								
37. Miscellaneous								
38. Professional Orgs								
39. RTNDA								
40. Other								
41.								
Subtotal								

DIRECTOR AND STAFF

CREW	ESTIMATED				ACTUAL			
	Days	Rate	O/T Hrs	Total	Days	Rate	O/T Hrs	Total
42. Director								
43. Preproduction								
44. Production								
45. Postproduction								
46. Assistant Director								
47. Preproduction								
48. Production								
49. Postproduction								
50. Director's Supplies								
51. Photocopying								
52. Telephone								
53. Postage								
54. Expenses								
55. Miscellaneous								
56.								
		Subtotal						

TALENT

DESCRIPTION	ESTIMATED				ACTUAL			
	Days	Rate	O/T Hrs	Total	Days	Rate	O/T Hrs	Total
57. Anchor No. ( )								
58. Preproduction								
59. Production								
60. Postproduction								
61. Weathercaster								
62. Preproduction								
63. Production								
64. Postproduction								
65. Sportscaster								
66. Preproduction								
67. Production								
68. Postproduction								
69. Editorialist								
70. Preproduction								
71. Production								
72. Postproduction								
73.								
74. Extra Talent								
75.								
		Subtotal						

BENEFITS

DESCRIPTION	TOTAL
76. Insurance Coverage	
77. Other	
78. Taxes	
Subtotal	

PRODUCTION FACILITY

DESCRIPTION	ESTIMATED				ACTUAL			
	Days	Rate	O/T Hrs	Total	Days	Rate	O/T Hrs	Total
79. Production Studio								
80. Studio Camera								
81. Studio Camera								
82. Studio Camera								
83. Studio Camera								
84. Teleprompter								
85. Floor Monitor								
86. Floor Monitor								
87.								
88.								
89. Control Room								
90. Production Switcher								
91. Digital Video Effects								
92. Still Store								
93.								
94. Intercom Network								
95.								
96. Character Generator								
97.								
98. Audio Control Board								
99. Cartridge Playback								
100. Cassette Playback								
101. Reel-to-Reel Playback								
102. Turntable								
103. Compact Disc Player								
104. Studio Foldback								
105.								
106. Master Control								
107. Record Deck No.( )								
108. Playback Deck No.( )								
109.								
110. Telecine								
111. 16mm								
112. 35mm								
113. Other								
114.								
115. Dressing Rooms								
116. Make-Up Facility								
117. Other								
	Subtotal							

PRODUCTION STAFF

CREW	ESTIMATED				ACTUAL			
	Days	Rate	O/T Hrs	Total	Days	Rate	O/T Hrs	Total
118. Technical Director								
119. Preproduction								
120. Production								
121. Postproduction								
122. Floor Director								
123. Preproduction								
124. Production								
125. Postproduction								
126. Production Assistant								
127. Preproduction								
128. Production								
129. Postproduction								
130. Teleprompter Operator								
131. Preproduction								
132. Production								
133. Postproduction								
134. Telecine Operator								
135. Preproduction								
136. Production								
137. Postproduction								
138. Graphic Artist								
139. Graphic Producer								
140. Videographer No.( )								
141. Video Editor No.( )								
142. Other Crew								
143. Miscellaneous								
144.								
		Subtotal						

CAMERAS, VIDEOTAPE RECORDING, VIDEO ENGINEERING

DESCRIPTION	ESTIMATED				ACTUAL			
	Days	Rate	O/T Hrs	Total	Days	Rate	O/T Hrs	Total
145. Camera Operator No.( )								
146. Preproduction								
147. Production								
148. Postproduction								
149. VTR Operator								
150. Preproduction								
151. Production								
152. Postproduction								
153. Video Engineer								
154. Preproduction								
155. Production								
156. Postproduction								
157. Other Crew								
158. Preproduction								
159. Production								
160. Postproduction								

CAMERAS, VIDEOTAPE RECORDING, AND VIDEO ENGINEERING (Con't)

DESCRIPTION	ESTIMATED				ACTUAL			
	Days	Rate	O/T Hrs	Total	Days	Rate	O/T Hrs	Total
161. Equipment Rental								
162. Equipment Purchases								
163. Maintenance/Repair								
164. Miscellaneous								
165.								
	Subtotal							

NEWS GATHERING SOURCES, MATERIALS

DESCRIPTION	ESTIMATED				ACTUAL			
	Days	Rate	O/T Hrs	Total	Days	Rate	O/T Hrs	Total
166. Wire Service								
167. UPI								
168. AP								
169. NewsNet								
170.								
171. Video News Service								
172.								
173. Audio News Service								
174.								
175. Videotape Library								
176.								
177. Newspapers								
178.								
179. News Magazine								
180.								
181. Electronic Newsroom								
182. Computer Hardware								
183.								
184.								
185. Computer Software								
186.								
187.								
188. Mail Subscription								
189.								
190. Telephone								
191. WATS Line								
192. International								
193.								
194. Monitoring Hardware								
195. Postage								
196. Federal Express								
197. UPS								
198. Other								
	Subtotal							

ENG NEWS GATHERING, EXPENSES

DESCRIPTION	ESTIMATED				ACTUAL			
	Days	Rate	O/T Hrs	Total	Days	Rate	O/T Hrs	Total
199. Maintenance/Engineer								
200. Checkout Personnel								
201.								
202. 3/4" Remote Kit No.( )								
203. ENG Camera								
204. Videotape Recorder								
205. Light Kit								
206. Microphones								
207. 1" Remote Kit No.( )								
208. ENG Camera								
209. Videotape Recorder								
210. Light Kit								
211. Microphones								
212. 1/2" Remote Kit No.( )								
213. ENG Camera								
214. Videotape Recorder								
215. Light Kit								
216. Microphones								
217.								
218. News Vehicle								
219.								
220. Two-way Telephone								
221.								
222.								
	Subtotal							

NEWS SET DESIGN, CONSTRUCTION, DECORATION, PROPERTIES

DESCRIPTION	ESTIMATED				ACTUAL			
	Days	Rate	O/T Hrs	Total	Days	Rate	O/T Hrs	Total
223. Set Design								
224. Artist								
225. Construction Labor								
226. Construction Materials								
227.								
228. Miscellaneous								
229.								
230. Set Decorator								
231. Preproduction								
232. Production								
233. Set Dressing Labor								
234. Set Properties								
235. Set Dressing Props								
236. Purchases								
237. Miscellaneous								
238.								
239.								
	Subtotal							

SET LIGHTING

DESCRIPTION	ESTIMATED				ACTUAL			
	Days	Rate	O/T Hrs	Total	Days	Rate	O/T Hrs	Total
240. Lighting Director								
241. Preproduction								
242. Production								
243. Postproduction								
244. Expendables								
245. (gels, etc.)								
246. Light Instruments								
247. 1 kw Spot No.( )								
248. 2 kw Spot No.( )								
249. kw Spot No.( )								
250. 1 kw Scoop No.( )								
251. 1 1/2 kw Scoop No.( )								
252. 2 kw Scoop No.( )								
253. kw Scoop No.( )								
254. Ellipsoidal Spotlight								
255. Broad/Softlight No.( )								
256. Strip/Cyc Light No.( )								
257.								
258. Equipment Rentals								
259. Equipment Purchases								
260. Miscellaneous								
261.								
	Subtotal							

AUDIO PRODUCTION

DESCRIPTION	ESTIMATED				ACTUAL			
	Days	Rate	O/T Hrs	Total	Days	Rate	O/T Hrs	Total
262. Audio Director								
263. Preproduction								
264. Production								
265. Postproduction								
266. Microphones								
267. Lavaliere No.( )								
268. Handheld No.( )								
269. Wireless No.( )								
270.								
271. Miscellaneous Labor								
272. Equipment Rentals								
273. Equipment Purchases								
274. Miscellaneous								
275.								
	Subtotal							

WARDROBE, MAKE-UP, HAIRSTYLING

DESCRIPTION	ESTIMATED				ACTUAL			
	Days	Rate	O/T Hrs	Total	Days	Rate	O/T Hrs	Total
276. Wardrobe Purchases								
277.								
278. Wardrobe Rentals								
279.								
280. Loss/Damage								
281. Cleaning								
282. Miscellaneous								
283.								
284. Hairstylist								
285. Hairstyling Supplies								
286.								
287. Make-up Supplies								
288.								
289. Miscellaneous								
290.								
	Subtotal							

VIDEOTAPE STOCK, FILM STOCK, PROCESSING

DESCRIPTION	ESTIMATED				ACTUAL			
	Days	Rate	O/T Hrs	Total	Days	Rate	O/T Hrs	Total
291. Videotape:								
1" (:) x ($)								
3/4" (:20) x ($)								
3/4" (:30) x ($)								
3/4" (:60) x ($)								
292.								
293. Film Stock								
294. 35mm								
295. 16mm								
296. Film Processing								
297.								
298. Miscellaneous								
	Subtotal							

POSTPRODUCTION EDITING

DESCRIPTION	ESTIMATED				ACTUAL			
	Days	Rate	O/T Hrs	Total	Days	Rate	O/T Hrs	Total
299. Editing Suite Rental								
300. Master Tape Stock								
301. SMPTE Coding								
302. Sound Effects								
303. Dupes ( ) x ($)per								
304. Miscellaneous								
305.								
	Subtotal							

MUSIC

DESCRIPTION	ESTIMATED				ACTUAL			
	Days	Rate	O/T Hrs	Total	Days	Rate	O/T Hrs	Total
306. Music Purchases								
307. Music Royalties								
308. Recording Facility								
309.								
310. Audio Recording Tape								
311.								
312. Miscellaneous								
313.								
	Subtotal							

COMMENTS

NEWSCAST FORMAT

MULTIPLE CAMERA VIDEO NEWS PRODUCTION

NEWSCAST SEGMENT	STORY SLUG	TIME	VTR	GPH	AUDIO	RUNNING/BACK TIME

Unit One
    vo/crt/lve   00:00 / 28:30

__:__ / __:__

Commercial Break   __:__   __:__ / __:__

Unit Two

__:__ / __:__

Commercial Break   __:__   __:__ / __:__

Unit Three

__:__ / __:__

Commercial Break   __:__   __:__ / __:__

Unit Four

__:__ / __:__

Commercial Break   __:__   __:__ / __:__

Unit Five

   28:30 / 00:00

NEWSCAST DESIGN

MULTIPLE CAMERA VIDEO NEWS PRODUCTION

News Director:	Newscast Title:
Executive Producer:	
News Producer:	Date: / /

| VIDEO CHOICES | STORYBOARD | AUDIO COPY |

SEGMENT 1

TIME

Opening shot
  Prerecorded video
  Studio set
  Video headlines

__:__

Music cart (up and under)

Title matte
  Computer generated title
  Character Generator title
  Video

__:__

Announcer: THIS IS [   ]

Talent intro
  Framing
  Zoom
  Character Generator
    lower third

__:__

Anchor 1: Hi. I'M [   ]

Anchor 2: ... AND I'M [   ]

  IN TODAY'S LEAD STORY ...
  HERE IS OUR REPORTER [   ]

Lead Story
  Anchor toss
  Reporter
  Reporter lower third
    live in studio
    vo
    live on location
    prerecorded

__:__

__:__

VIDEO CHOICES | STORYBOARD | AUDIO COPY

TIME

Bumper
  Colored background
  Character Generator
  Video tease
  Talent tease
  _____

SEGMENT 2

__:__

__:__

__:__

__:__

__:__

__:__

VIDEO CHOICES　　　　　STORYBOARD　　　　　AUDIO COPY

SEGMENT

TIME

__:__

__:__

__:__

__:__

__:__

__:__

NEWS SET DESIGN

MULTIPLE CAMERA VIDEO NEWS PRODUCTION

News Director: Date: /   /
Executive Producer: Newscast: ☐Morning ☐Noon
News Producer: ☐Early ☐Evening ☐Late

Bird's Eye View (17 units x 23 units)

Front View (10 units x 23 units)

STUDIO CAMERA BLOCKING PLOT

MULTIPLE CAMERA VIDEO NEWS PRODUCTION

Studio Director:

Date: /   /

Newscast:

Set:

Lighting
- ☐ _____
- ☐ _____
- ☐ _____
- ☐ _____

Audio
- ☐ _____
- ☐ _____
- ☐ _____

Bird's Eye Floor Plan

Cameras /Properties/Blocking

Description:

Cameras/Movement/Properties

In-cue

Out-cue

Comments:

STUDIO CAMERA SHOT LIST

MULTIPLE CAMERA VIDEO NEWS PRODUCTION

Camera Operator:
Camera: C1 C2 C3
Date: /   /

Newscast:
Newscast Production Date: /   /
Set:

SHOT No.	CAMERA FRAMING	TALENT	CAMERA MOVEMENT	SPECIAL INSTRUCTIONS

NEWS SET AUDIO PLOT

MULTIPLE CAMERA VIDEO NEWS PRODUCTION

Audio Director:

Director:

     Approval ☐

Date: / /

Newscast Title:

Set:

Microphone
- ☐ Directional
- ☐ Wireless
- ☐ Lavaliere
- ☐ _____

Microphone Support
- ☐ _____
- ☐ _____

Sound Effects
- ☐ Foldback
- ☐ _____

Bird's Eye Floor Plan

Cameras /Properties/Blocking
Microphone Support(s)/Cable Run(s)

Description:

Cameras/Movement/Properties

In-cue	Opening Cart/Closing Cart Bumper	Out-cue	Opening Cart/Closing Cart Bumper

Rights/Clearance Required:

NEWS SET LIGHTING PLOT
MULTIPLE CAMERA VIDEO NEWS PRODUCTION

Lighting Director:

Director:

    Approval ☐

Newscast:

Set:

Date: /   /

Lighting

☐ _____
☐ _____
☐ _____
☐ _____

Lighting
    Change
☐ Yes
☐ No

Bird's Eye Floor Plan

Cameras/Properties/Blocking

Description:

Cameras/Movement/Properties

Lighting Instruments
    Key Lights:
    Fill Lights:
    Soft Lights:

Lighting Accessories
    Barn Doors:
    Flags:
    Gobo:

Filters
    Spun Glass:
    Gels:
    Scrims:

Newscast Logo

Other Requirements

In-cue

Opening/Closing
Bumper

Out-cue

Opening/Closing
Bumper

TALENT AUDITION

MULTIPLE CAMERA VIDEO NEWSCAST PRODUCTION

News Director:	Newscast:

Position:
☐ Anchor　　☐ Weathercaster　　☐ Sportscaster　　☐ Feature Producer/Reporter

Name:	Telephone:
Address:	Home ( )　　-
City:	Work ( )　　-
State:　　　　　　Zip Code:	Birthdate:　　/　　/

Availability	Unavailability
Dates:　　　　　　Hours:	Dates:　　　　　　Hours:

Personal Data:　Height　　　　　Weight　　　　　Ethnicity:
　Hat Size:　　　　Shoe Size:　　　　Waist Measurement:　　　Chest Measurement:
　In Seam:　　　　Shirt/Blouse Size:　　　　　Suit/Dress Size:

Agent:
Union Affiliation:

Please explain your interest in this production:

Please list other experiences that you feel qualify you for the position for which you are
　auditioning:

Make any additional comments about your qualifications for this position:

PLEASE ATTACH YOUR RESUME AND PHOTO TO THIS FORM, OR LIST PREVIOUS EXPERIENCE
AND/OR DRAMA TRAINING ON THE REVERSE SIDE OF THIS FORM.

NEWS BEAT/FUTURE FILE
MULTIPLE CAMERA VIDEO NEWS PRODUCTION

Compiler: Source: Date: /   /

Organization Title/Beat:

General Offices/Address:
     City: State: Zip Code:
Telephone No. (   )   -

Public Relations Officer:
     Telephone No. (   )   -   Extension:
Press Officer:
     Telephone No. (   )   -   Extension:
Communication Office:
     Telephone No. (   )   -   Extension:

Organizational Goals/Objectives:

ON FILE
- ☐ Press Releases   ☐ _____   ☐ _____   ☐ _____
- ☐ Videotape   ☐ _____   ☐ _____   ☐ _____
- ☐ Still Photos   ☐ _____   ☐ _____   ☐ _____
- ☐ 35mm Slides   ☐ _____   ☐ _____   ☐ _____
- ☐ Logo   ☐ _____   ☐ _____   ☐ _____

Entered into Database
- ☐ Updated   Date: /   /   Initialed:
- ☐ Updated   Date: /   /   Initialed:
- ☐ Updated   Date: /   /   Initialed:

NEWSCAST ASSIGNMENT
MULTIPLE CAMERA VIDEO NEWS PRODUCTION

Reporter/Feature Producer: _____   Today's Date: /   /
Videographer: _____   Newscast Date: /   /

☐ Story Assignment: deadline   /   /   air date   /   /
☐ Proposal   ☐ Approved
☐ Recommendation Only: ☐ FYI   ☐ initiative   ☐ personal interest

NEWS STORY   News Slug _____

   Event:

   Date: /   /   Time: ___ : ___   Place:
   Travel directions:

   Story description:

   Background:

   Contact person: Phone: (   )   -

   Additional leads:

FEATURE PACKAGE   Title: _____   ☐ Unit   ☐ Series
   Idea: No. ☐

   Objective(s):

   Location(s):

   Contact(s):   Phone: (   )   -

   Background/Leads:

☐ SEE ATTACHED   ☐ LET'S MEET ON THIS

GRAPHIC DESIGN REQUEST
MULTIPLE CAMERA VIDEO NEWS PRODUCTION

Reporter/Producer:	Date Requested: / /
News Producer:	Newscast:
Graphic Artist/Producer:	Deadline: / / ___:___ AM/PM

Graphic No.	Story Slug/Feature Title	Notes Content description	Status
			☐ available ☐ unavailable ☐ to be created
			☐ available ☐ unavailable ☐ to be created
			☐ available ☐ unavailable ☐ to be created
			☐ available ☐ unavailable ☐ to be created
			☐ available ☐ unavailable ☐ to be created
			☐ available ☐ unavailable ☐ to be created
			☐ available ☐ unavailable ☐ to be created
			☐ available ☐ unavailable ☐ to be created
			☐ available ☐ unavailable ☐ to be created
			☐ available ☐ unavailable ☐ to be created
			☐ available ☐ unavailable ☐ to be created
			☐ available ☐ unavailable ☐ to be created
			☐ available ☐ unavailable ☐ to be created
			☐ available ☐ unavailable ☐ to be created
			☐ available ☐ unavailable ☐ to be created
			☐ available ☐ unavailable ☐ to be created
			☐ available ☐ unavailable ☐ to be created
			☐ available ☐ unavailable ☐ to be created
			☐ available ☐ unavailable ☐ to be created

EMERGENCY SERVICES CALL LOG
MULTIPLE CAMERA VIDEO NEWS PRODUCTION

Assignment Editor: _____   Week of   /   /

NAME	CODE	PREFIX	NUMBER	SUNDAY	MONDAY	TUESDAY	WEDNESDAY	THURSDAY	FRIDAY	SATURDAY

MUNICIPALITY

Fire

Police

City

County

State

Hospital

MUNICIPALITY

Fire

Police

City

County

State

Hospital

MUNICIPALITY

Fire

Police

City

County

State

Hospital

MUNICIPALITY

Fire

Police

City

County

State

Hospital

REMOTE ASSIGNMENT

MULTIPLE CAMERA VIDEO NEWS PRODUCTION

Assignment Editor: Newscast:

News Producer: Date: /   /

STORY/ FEATURE	REPORTER/PRODUCER	VIDEOGRAPHER	CAMERA UNIT	VEHICLE	DESTINATION	DEPART	RETURN
						: am pm	: am pm
						: am pm	: am pm
						: am pm	: am pm
						: am pm	: am pm
						: am pm	: am pm
						: am pm	: am pm
						: am pm	: am pm
						: am pm	: am pm
						: am pm	: am pm
						: am pm	: am pm
						: am pm	: am pm
						: am pm	: am pm
						: am pm	: am pm
						: am pm	: am pm
						: am pm	: am pm
						: am pm	: am pm
						: am pm	: am pm
						: am pm	: am pm
						: am pm	: am pm
						: am pm	: am pm
						: am pm	: am pm
						: am pm	: am pm
						: am pm	: am pm
						: am pm	: am pm
						: am pm	: am pm
						: am pm	: am pm
						: am pm	: am pm
						: am pm	: am pm
						: am pm	: am pm
						: am pm	: am pm
						: am pm	: am pm
						: am pm	: am pm

EDITOR/EDITING RESERVATION

MULTIPLE CAMERA VIDEO NEWS PRODUCTION

Assignment Editor: Newscast:

News Producer: Date: /   /

STORY/ FEATURE	REPORTER/PRODUCER	VIDEO EDITOR	EDITING SUITE	SPECIAL EFFECTS	SPECIAL INSTRUCTIONS	BEGIN SESSION	END SESSION
						: am pm	: am pm
						: am pm	: am pm
						: am pm	: am pm
						: am pm	: am pm
						: am pm	: am pm
						: am pm	: am pm
						: am pm	: am pm
						: am pm	: am pm
						: am pm	: am pm
						: am pm	: am pm
						: am pm	: am pm
						: am pm	: am pm
						: am pm	: am pm
						: am pm	: am pm
						: am pm	: am pm
						: am pm	: am pm
						: am pm	: am pm
						: am pm	: am pm
						: am pm	: am pm
						: am pm	: am pm
						: am pm	: am pm
						: am pm	: am pm
						: am pm	: am pm
						: am pm	: am pm
						: am pm	: am pm
						: am pm	: am pm
						: am pm	: am pm
						: am pm	: am pm
						: am pm	: am pm
						: am pm	: am pm
						: am pm	: am pm
						: am pm	: am pm

VIDEO PRODUCTION CALENDAR
MULTIPLE CAMERA VIDEO NEWS PRODUCTION

News Producer: _____ Newscast: _____

Producer	Videographer	Video Editor	Assign.	Treatment	Preprod Script	Location	Shooting Schedule	Editing Date	Deadline
			/ /	/ /	/ /		/ /	/ /	/ /
			/ /	/ /	/ /		/ /	/ /	/ /
			/ /	/ /	/ /		/ /	/ /	/ /
			/ /	/ /	/ /		/ /	/ /	/ /
			/ /	/ /	/ /		/ /	/ /	/ /
			/ /	/ /	/ /		/ /	/ /	/ /
			/ /	/ /	/ /		/ /	/ /	/ /
			/ /	/ /	/ /		/ /	/ /	/ /
			/ /	/ /	/ /		/ /	/ /	/ /

▢	▢	▢	▢	▢	▢	▢
▢	▢	▢	▢	▢	▢	▢
▢	▢	▢	▢	▢	▢	▢
▢	▢	▢	▢	▢	▢	▢
▢	▢	▢	▢	▢	▢	▢

NOTES

PACKAGE TREATMENT
MULTIPLE CAMERA VIDEO NEWS PRODUCTION

Feature Producer:	Proposed Title:
Videographer:	Proposed Length: :
	Proposed Shooting Date: / /
Date: / /	Proposed Completion Date: / /
Location(s):	
	Page of

Production Statement

Communication Goals and Objectives of the Package; Most Important Questions

Package Treatment

(Continue on reverse side.)

TELEVISION SCRIPT

MULTIPLE CAMERA VIDEO NEWS PRODUCTION

Feature Producer:	Package Title:
Videographer:	Length: : Date: / / Page of

VIDEO	AUDIO

VIDEO	AUDIO

VIDEO SCRIPT/STORYBOARD

MULTIPLE CAMERA VIDEO NEWS PRODUCTION

Feature Producer: Package Title:

Videographer: Length: :
                                           Date: /   /
                                           Page   of

VIDEO	AUDIO

| VIDEO | AUDIO |

GRAPHIC DESIGN

MULTIPLE CAMERA VIDEO NEWS PRODUCTION

News Producer:

Assignment Editor:

Reporter/Writer:

Feature Producer:

Graphic Artist/Producer:

Date: / /

Newscast Date: / /

Deadline: / /

____:____ AM/PM

Graphic No. ☐

Story Slug/Feature Title:

Concept:

Text:

Image Design:

Graphic No. ☐

Story Slug/Feature Title:

Concept:

Text:

Image Design:

Graphic No. ☐

Story Slug/Feature Title:

Concept:

Text:

Image Design:

Graphic No. ☐

Story Slug/Feature Title:
Concept:

Text:

Image Design:

Graphic No. ☐

Story Slug/Feature Title:
Concept:

Text:

Image Design:

Graphic No. ☐

Story Slug/Feature Title:
Concept:

Text:

Image Design:

Graphic No. ☐

Story Slug/Feature Title:
Concept:

Text:

Image Design:

SCRIPT BREAKDOWN

MULTIPLE CAMERA VIDEO NEWS PRODUCTION

Feature Producer:

Videographer:

Package Title:

Length: :
Script Length: pages
Page   of
Date: /   /

SCRIPT PAGES	NO. OF SCRIPT LINES	INT/ EXT	TIME	SETTING	LOCATION	TALENT	SHOOT-ING ORDER

REMOTE CAMERA SHOT LIST

MULTIPLE CAMERA VIDEO NEWS PRODUCTION

Feature Producer:

Package Title:

Videographer:

Date: / /

Page of

LOCATION	SHOT						CONTENT NOTES
	NO.	MASTER	CUT-IN	CUT-AWAY	FRAMING	MOTION	

LOCATION	SHOT						CONTENT NOTES
	NO.	MASTER	CUT-IN	CUT-AWAY	FRAMING	MOTION	

LOCATION SITE SURVEY

MULTIPLE CAMERA VIDEO NEWS PRODUCTION

Feature Producer:	Package Title:
	Date: / /

Newscast: | Assigned Deadline: / /

Location: | Site Identification:
Local Contact Person: | Comments:
  Name:
  Title:
  Address:
  City: State:
  Phone No.: (   )   -
Facilities Personnel: Comments:
  Name:
  Position Title:
  Address:
  City: State:
  Phone No.: (   )   -

LIGHTING PROBLEMS DEFINED

Light contrast ratios	Existing light control
Lighting intensity	Lighting use
Ceiling height	Floor description
Windows/Compass direction	Special consideration

POWER PROBLEMS DEFINED	
Number of power outlets	Number of outlet prongs
Number of separate circuits	Location of circuit breakers
Types of fuses	Portable generator need

AUDIO PROBLEMS DEFINED	
Interior environmental sounds	Exterior environmental sounds
Ceiling composition	Floor covering composition
Wall composition	

CAST AND CREW NEEDS	
Restroom facilities	Eating facilities
Green room availability	Make-up facilities
Parking arrangements	Loading/unloading restrictions
Freight elevator	Hardware store

CIVIL EMERGENCY SERVICES

Police station	Fire station

LOCATION SECURITY AND EQUIPMENT SAFETY

Facility security	Equipment safe storage
Personnel valuables security	Overnight storage/security

OTHER RELEVANT INFORMATION

Public area power source	Traffic control
Clearance/Insurance needed	Exterior compass direction
Photographs taken	Location environment drawing/map
Other information:	

OTHER COMMENTS/OBSERVATIONS

PRODUCTION SCHEDULE

MULTIPLE CAMERA VIDEO NEWS PRODUCTION

Feature Producer:	Package Title:
Videographer:	Date: / / Page of

SHOOTING DAY 1　　　　　　　　　　　　　　　**RAIN DATE**

_____, _____, _____　　___/___/___
　(Weekday)　　　　　(Month)　　　(Day)

Location Site:_____ Location Map No._____

Address: _____

　　　City_____ State _____

Location Host:_____
Phone No.: (___)___-_____

Crew call:___:___ AM/PM
　Address:_____

Talent call:___:___ AM/PM
　Address:_____

Set-up:___:___ to ___:___　　　Projected Strike Time:___:___

SHOOT ORDER UNITS	SCRIPT PAGES	SETTING	APPROX. TIME	CAST	ACTION PROPERTIES
			: to :		
			: to :		
			: to :		
			: to :		
			: to :		

Comments:

EQUIPMENT CHECKLIST

MULTIPLE CAMERA VIDEO NEWS PRODUCTION

Feature Producer: Package Title:

Videographer:

Location(s):   Date: /   /

Avl   Pch   Rnt   Avl   Pch   Rnt

CAMERA
- Video Camera
- Lenses
- Filters
- AC/DC Monitor
- Lg Screen Monitor
- _____

RECORDER
- Videotape Recorder
- _____
- _____

TRIPOD
- Tripod w/Head
- Camera Head Adapter
- Dolly
- _____

TEST EQUIPMENT
- Waveform Monitor
- Vectorscope
- Grey Scale
- Registration Chart
- White Card
- Headphones
- _____

AUDIO
- Shotgun Microphone
- Lavaliere Microphone
- Hand-held Microphone
- Fishpole
- Wind screens

AUDIO (continued)
- Mixer
- Adapter plugs
- Earphone
- Headphones
- _____

POWER SUPPLIES
- Batteries for Camera
- Batteries for Recorder
- Batteries for Monitor
- AC Power Converter
- Microphone Batteries

LIGHTING
- Light Kit
- Soft Light Kit
- Barn Doors
- Spun Glass Filters
- Blue Gels
- Orange Gels
- Screens
- Scrims
- ND Filters
- Aluminum Foil
- Wooden Clothespins
- Light Meter
- Reflector
- Spare Bulbs
- Flags
- _____

Avl Pch Rnt

CABLES

☐ ☐ ☐ Multipin Cable Camera
          to Recorder
☐ ☐ ☐ Video Cable Camera
          to Recorder
☐ ☐ ☐ Video Cable Camera
          to Waveform Monitor/
          Scope
☐ ☐ ☐ Video Cable Scope to
          Monitor
☐ ☐ ☐ Audio Mixer Cable to
          Recorder
☐ ☐ ☐ Audio Extension Cables
          _____

MISCELLANEOUS

☐ ☐ ☐ Videotape
☐ ☐ ☐ Teleprompter
☐ ☐ ☐ Teleprompter Script
☐ ☐ ☐ Cue Card Paper
☐ ☐ ☐ Duct Tape
☐ ☐ ☐ Masking Tape
☐ ☐ ☐ Spare Fuses
☐ ☐ ☐ Tool Kit
☐ ☐ ☐ Stopwatch
☐ ☐ ☐ Slate
☐ ☐ ☐ Chalk
☐ ☐ ☐ Eraser
☐ ☐ ☐ Bullhorn
☐ ☐ ☐ Walkie-Talkie
☐ ☐ ☐ Dulling Spray
☐ ☐ ☐ Talent Release Forms
☐ ☐ ☐ Step Ladder
☐ ☐ ☐ Lens Cleaner and Tissue

Avl Pch Rnt

MISCELLANEOUS (continued)

☐ ☐ ☐ Sewing Kit
☐ ☐ ☐ Paper, Pens, Felt Markers
☐ ☐ ☐ Rope
☐ ☐ ☐ Barrier Cones
☐ ☐ ☐ Poster Board
☐ ☐ ☐ Flashlight
☐ ☐ ☐ Scissors
☐ ☐ ☐ 100' Power Cords
☐ ☐ ☐ Staple Gun and Staples
☐ ☐ ☐ Power Outlet Boxes
☐ ☐ ☐ _____
☐ ☐ ☐ _____
☐ ☐ ☐ _____
☐ ☐ ☐ _____
☐ ☐ ☐ _____
☐ ☐ ☐ _____
☐ ☐ ☐ _____
☐ ☐ ☐ _____
☐ ☐ ☐ _____
☐ ☐ ☐ _____
☐ ☐ ☐ _____
☐ ☐ ☐ _____
☐ ☐ ☐ _____
☐ ☐ ☐ _____

REMOTE LOG

MULTIPLE CAMERA VIDEO NEWS PRODUCTION

Feature Producer:

Videographer:

Package Title:
Location:
Date: /   /
Page   of

VTR COUNTER/ TIMER/CODE	LOCATION	TALENT	TAKE NO.	GOOD/ NO GOOD	VIDEO/AUDIO

TALENT RELEASE FORM

MULTIPLE CAMERA VIDEO NEWS PRODUCTION

Talent Name: _____
(Please Print)

Project Title: _____

For value received and without further consideration, I hereby consent to the use of all photographs, videotapes or film taken of me, and/or recordings made of my voice, and/or written extraction, in whole or in part, of such recordings or musical performance

at _____ on _____ 19___
(Recording Location)   (Month)   (Day)   (Year)

by_____ for_____
(Producer)   (Producing Organization)

and/or others with its consent, for the purposes of illustration, advertising, or publication in any manner.

Talent Name_____
(Signature)

Address_____ City_____

State _____ Zip Code _____

Date:___/___/___

If the subject is a minor under the laws of the state where modeling, acting, or performing is done:

Guardian _____ Guardian _____
(Signature)   (Please Print)

Address _____ City _____

State _____ Zip Code _____

Date:___/___/___

EDITING WORK SHEET

MULTIPLE CAMERA VIDEO NEWS PRODUCTION

Feature Producer:	Package Title:
	Date: / /
Reporter/Writer:	Audio: Channel 1
	Audio: Channel 2
	Page of

TAPE No.	VTR CNTR		NOTES	SEGMENT CLOCK TIME
	CLOCK			
	SMPTE			
	IN	OUT		
				:
				:
				:
				:
				:
				:
				:
				:
				:
				:
				:
				:
				:
				:
				:
				:
				:
				:
				:
				:
				:
				:
				:
				:
				:
				:
				:

T A P E No.	VTR CNTR CLOCK SMPTE		NOTES	SEGMENT CLOCK TIME
	IN	OUT		
				:
				:
				:
				:
				:
				:
				:
				:
				:
				:
				:
				:
				:
				:
				:
				:
				:
				:
				:
				:
				:
				:
				:
				:
				:
				:
				:
				:
				:
				:
				:
				:
				:
				:
				:

EDITING CUE SHEET

MULTIPLE CAMERA VIDEO NEWS PRODUCTION

Feature Producer:

Reporter/Writer:

Package Title:
Date: /   /
Audio: Channel 1
Audio: Channel 2
Page   of

TAPE No.	VTR CNTR CLOCK SMPTE IN	OUT	NOTES	SEGMENT CLOCK TIME
			IN-CUE	:
			OUT-CUE	
			IN-CUE	:
			OUT-CUE	
			IN-CUE	:
			OUT-CUE	
			IN-CUE	:
			OUT-CUE	
			IN-CUE	:
			OUT-CUE	
			IN-CUE	:
			OUT-CUE	
			IN-CUE	:
			OUT-CUE	
			IN-CUE	:
			OUT-CUE	
			IN-CUE	:
			OUT-CUE	
			IN-CUE	:
			OUT-CUE	
			IN-CUE	:
			OUT-CUE	
			IN-CUE	:
			OUT-CUE	
			IN-CUE	:
			OUT-CUE	
			IN-CUE	:
			OUT-CUE	
			IN-CUE	:
			OUT-CUE	

T A P E No.	VTR CNTR CLOCK SMPTE		NOTES	SEGMENT CLOCK TIME
	IN	OUT		
			IN-CUE	
			OUT-CUE	:
			IN-CUE	
			OUT-CUE	:
			IN-CUE	
			OUT-CUE	:
			IN-CUE	
			OUT-CUE	:
			IN-CUE	
			OUT-CUE	:
			IN-CUE	
			OUT-CUE	:
			IN-CUE	
			OUT-CUE	:
			IN-CUE	
			OUT-CUE	:
			IN-CUE	
			OUT-CUE	:
			IN-CUE	
			OUT-CUE	:
			IN-CUE	
			OUT-CUE	:
			IN-CUE	
			OUT-CUE	:
			IN-CUE	
			OUT-CUE	:
			IN-CUE	
			OUT-CUE	:
			IN-CUE	
			OUT-CUE	:
			IN-CUE	
			OUT-CUE	:
			IN-CUE	
			OUT-CUE	:
			IN-CUE	
			OUT-CUE	:

EDITED MASTER CLIPSHEET
MULTIPLE CAMERA VIDEO NEWS PRODUCTION

Feature Producer: Package Title/Story Slug:
Reporter/Writer: Date: /   /
Video Editor: Audio: Channel 1 ☐   2 ☐   Mixed ☐

Package Title/Story Slug:
_____

Length: (first audio to final audio)
_____ : _____

Out-cue:
_____

Character Generator Copy: Notes
    Videotape/Film Credit   In ___:___
                              Out ___:___

           _____

    Reporter Lower Third   In ___:___
                              Out ___:___

           _____

    Interviewee/Actuality Lower Third   In ___:___
                              Out ___:___

           _____
           _____

    Interviewee/Actuality Lower Third   In ___:___
                              Out ___:___

           _____
           _____

    Voice of   In ___:___
                              Out ___:___

           _____
           _____

Character Generator Copy (continued)   Notes

    Transcription #1   In ___:___
                                      Out ___:___

    Transcription #2   In ___:___
                                      Out ___:___

    Trade Credit   In ___:___
                                      Out ___:___

    Video Credits   In ___:___
                                      Out ___:___

_____
                           Producer

_____
                       Videographer

_____
                       Video Editor

GRAPHICS SUMMARY RUNDOWN
MULTIPLE CAMERA VIDEO NEWS PRODUCTION

Graphic Artist/Producer:

To: ☐ News Producer
     ☐ Telecine Operator
     ☐ Technical Director
     ☐ Assistant Director
     ☐ _____

Newscast Date: /   /

Newscast:
     ☐ Morning
     ☐ Noon
     ☐ Early   ☐ Evening   ☐ Late

Newscast Order	Story Slug / Feature Title	Graphics Description	Screen Position	Source
			☐ matte right ☐ matte left ☐ full screen	☐ telecine ☐ still store ☐ freeze frame ☐ videotape
			☐ matte right ☐ matte left ☐ full screen	☐ telecine ☐ still store ☐ freeze frame ☐ videotape
			☐ matte right ☐ matte left ☐ full screen	☐ telecine ☐ still store ☐ freeze frame ☐ videotape
			☐ matte right ☐ matte left ☐ full screen	☐ telecine ☐ still store ☐ freeze frame ☐ videotape
			☐ matte right ☐ matte left ☐ full screen	☐ telecine ☐ still store ☐ freeze frame ☐ videotape
			☐ matte right ☐ matte left ☐ full screen	☐ telecine ☐ still store ☐ freeze frame ☐ videotape
			☐ matte right ☐ matte left ☐ full screen	☐ telecine ☐ still store ☐ freeze frame ☐ videotape
			☐ matte right ☐ matte left ☐ full screen	☐ telecine ☐ still store ☐ freeze frame ☐ videotape
			☐ matte right ☐ matte left ☐ full screen	☐ telecine ☐ still store ☐ freeze frame ☐ videotape
			☐ matte right ☐ matte left ☐ full screen	☐ telecine ☐ still store ☐ freeze frame ☐ videotape
			☐ matte right ☐ matte left ☐ full screen	☐ telecine ☐ still store ☐ freeze frame ☐ videotape

Graphics Summary Rundown (continued)			Page	of

Newscast Order	Story Slug / Feature Title	Graphics Description	Screen Position	Source
			☐ matte right ☐ matte left ☐ full screen	☐ telecine ☐ still store ☐ freeze frame ☐ videotape
			☐ matte right ☐ matte left ☐ full screen	☐ telecine ☐ still store ☐ freeze frame ☐ videotape
			☐ matte right ☐ matte left ☐ full screen	☐ telecine ☐ still store ☐ freeze frame ☐ videotape
			☐ matte right ☐ matte left ☐ full screen	☐ telecine ☐ still store ☐ freeze frame ☐ videotape
			☐ matte right ☐ matte left ☐ full screen	☐ telecine ☐ still store ☐ freeze frame ☐ videotape
			☐ matte right ☐ matte left ☐ full screen	☐ telecine ☐ still store ☐ freeze frame ☐ videotape
			☐ matte right ☐ matte left ☐ full screen	☐ telecine ☐ still store ☐ freeze frame ☐ videotape
			☐ matte right ☐ matte left ☐ full screen	☐ telecine ☐ still store ☐ freeze frame ☐ videotape
			☐ matte right ☐ matte left ☐ full screen	☐ telecine ☐ still store ☐ freeze frame ☐ videotape
			☐ matte right ☐ matte left ☐ full screen	☐ telecine ☐ still store ☐ freeze frame ☐ videotape
			☐ matte right ☐ matte left ☐ full screen	☐ telecine ☐ still store ☐ freeze frame ☐ videotape
			☐ matte right ☐ matte left ☐ full screen	☐ telecine ☐ still store ☐ freeze frame ☐ videotape
			☐ matte right ☐ matte left ☐ full screen	☐ telecine ☐ still store ☐ freeze frame ☐ videotape
			☐ matte right ☐ matte left ☐ full screen	☐ telecine ☐ still store ☐ freeze frame ☐ videotape
			☐ matte right ☐ matte left ☐ full screen	☐ telecine ☐ still store ☐ freeze frame ☐ videotape

CHARACTER GENERATOR COPY

MULTIPLE CAMERA VIDEO NEWS PRODUCTION

Date: /   /   NEWSCAST: ☐ Morning ☐ Noon ☐ Early ☐ Evening ☐ Late

Production Assistant:

VIDEOTAPE LEADER

SLATE

Title: [_____]
Producers: [_____]
[_____] [_____]
Director: [_____]
Length: :
Taping Date: /   /
Air Date: /   /

Record No.
[____]

ACTUALITY LOWER THIRD

Record No.
[____]

"VOICE OF" CREDIT

Voice of

Record No.
[____]

SEGMENT 1   OPENING

TALENT LOWER THIRD

[_____] [_____]

Anchors

Record No.
[____]

REPORTER LOWER THIRD

[_____]

Reporting

Record No.
[____]

■ File tape

VIDEO/FILM CREDIT

Record No.
[____]

■ Courtesy of
[_____]

COURTESY CREDIT

Record No.
[____]

SEGMENT 1 (continued)

Record No.

Record No.

BUMPER

Record No.

Record No.

SEGMENT 2

REPORTER
LOWER
THIRD

Reporting

Record No.

Record No.

Record No.

Record No.

SEGMENT ☐

Record No.

Record No.

Record No.

Record No.

Record No.

Record No.

Record No.

Record No.

CLOSING CREDITS

Video Engineer
_____

Videotape Recording
_____

Lighting Director

Telecine
_____
Record No.

Videographers
_____
_____

Feature Producers
_____
Record No.

Studio Camera Operators
_____
_____

Studio Prompter Operator

Floor Director
_____
Record No.

Script Editor
_____
_____

Graphic Artist/Producer

Reporters
_____
Record No.

Audio Director
_____

Production Assistant

Assistant Director
_____

Technical Director
_____
Record No.

News Producer
_____

Assignment Editor

Executive News Producer
_____

News Director
_____
Record No.

Director
_____

Videotape Editors
_____
Record No.

Additional videotape
supplied by
_____

Copyright 1991
Record No.

VIDEO SOURCES

MULTIPLE CAMERA VIDEO NEWS PRODUCTION

Videotape Recorder Operator:

To: ☐ Technical Director
    ☐ Assistant Director
    ☐ Telecine Operator
    ☐ Video Engineer
    ☐ Audio Director
    ☐ _____

Newscast Date: /   /

Newscast:
    ☐ Morning
    ☐ Noon
    ☐ Early   ☐ Evening   ☐ Late

Newscast Segment	Story/ Feature	Graphics Source			B-Roll Source		Audio Source			Record VTR
#	slug/title	cine	ss	vtr#	vtr#	vtr#	vtr#	cart	live	#

FORMAT/RUNDOWN SHEET
MULTIPLE CAMERA VIDEO NEWS PRODUCTION

NEWSCAST SEGMENT	STORY SLUG	TIME	VID	GPH	AUDIO	RUNNING/BACK TIME

Unit One

vo/crt/lve 00:00 / 28:30

__:__ / __:__

Commercial Break __:__ __:__ / __:__

Unit Two

__:__ / __:__

Commercial Break __:__ __:__ / __:__

Unit Three

__:__ / __:__

Commercial Break __:__ __:__ / __:__

Unit Four

__:__ / __:__

Commercial Break __:__ __:__ / __:__

Unit Five

28:30 / 00:00

Chapter 4

Description and Glossary for Studio Production Organizing Forms

INTRODUCTION

A barometer to successful television production is the degree to which producing and production tasks are accomplished and the extent to which producing and production tasks are *successfully* accomplished. Equally important to successful accomplishment of those tasks is the knowledge and awareness of the details necessary at each newscast producing and production task stage.

This chapter presents a description and glossary of terms for successful newscast production task accomplishment. These descriptions and glossaries are presented in terms of the organizing forms in Chapter 3. Each organizing form is presented here by title, the particular production process to which it refers, the producing and/or production personnel responsible for the completion of the form and the tasks, and a description of the purpose of the form and of the objective in using the form.

Not all organizing forms are necessary or even required in every newscast production. They are selective and designed to be used as needed. Those forms that organize and assist in accomplishing a newscast producing or production task should be tried for the ease and thoroughness with which they organize a task. Those forms that are redundant to a particular newscast production should be ignored. The forms are meant to be helpful, not a stumbling block, to newscast production.

DESCRIPTION AND GLOSSARY

- **Production Budget Form**

Production process   Newscast preproduction

Responsibility   News director

Purpose   To realistically estimate all possible costs of the studio newscast from preproduction through postproduction.

Objective   The budget form is a blank model of a budget for the production of a studio newscast. The form is meant to organize as many facets of multiple camera news production as can be anticipated into estimated expenses and, after production, into actual expenses. The form suggests costs involved in preproduction, including, for example, news wire services. It suggests possible cost items across the spectrum of studio video production, personnel, equipment, labor, time, and materials.

The form should be used to suggest expenses and to call attention to possible hidden costs before production begins.

General comments on the use of the budget form
The form should be studied for line items that might pertain to a proposed multiple camera news production. Only applicable line items need to be considered. Use the suggestion of line items to weigh as many foreseeable real costs as possible for the project.

Note that all sections of the budget are summarized on the front page of the form. The subtotal of costs from the individual sections are brought forward to be listed in the summary.

Some costs are calculated by the number of days employed, the hourly rate of pay, and overtime hours. Other costs are calculated by the number of items or people and the allotted amount of money per day for the item or person. The cost of materials is calculated by the amount of materials times the cost of a unit.

Most cost entry columns of this budget form are labeled,

"Days, Rate, O/T (overtime) Hrs, Total." For those line items that do not involve day and rate, the total column alone should be used.

Projected costs to be applied to the budget can be determined from a number of sources. One source of equipment rental and production costs is the rate card of a local video production facility. Salary estimates and talent fees can be estimated from the going rates of relevant services of equivalent professionals or from their agencies. The Radio-Television News Directors Association magazine publication *Communicator* lists salaries for above-the-line news production personnel annually. Cost quotations can be requested in phone calls to providers of services and materials. Travel costs can be obtained by a phone call to a travel agency or an airline company. Preparing a good budget is going to involve a lot of time and research.

Glossary

News director The name of the news director responsible for budget construction is entered here.

Executive Producer The name of the executive producer who administers the budget on a day-to-day basis is recorded in this entry.

Date This is the date of the preparation of the production budget.

Newscast The title for the newscast being budgeted should be entered here.

Newscast Length The length of the budgeted newscast should be recorded here.

Frequency: Daily/Weekly/Other The production and telecast frequency of the budgeted newscast should be indicated here. The evaluation of the budget will obviously differ between that for a daily newscast and one for a weekly.

Preproduction Time per Newscast: Hours Estimate the number of hours needed to complete the necessary preproduction stage. This estimate includes time on all preproduction stages (news gathering, video producing, script writing, and production) for all producers and editors involved in preproduction.

No. Studio Production Day/Hours Estimate the number of days and hours for which the studio or control room facilities may be needed in the production of the newscast. This time estimate accounts for all in-studio videotaping (e.g., talent on a set) and the use of the control room switcher or character generator for postproduction effects.

Postproduction Time per Newscast: Hours Estimate the number of hours that will be spent in postproduction completing the master tape. This entry presupposes that the newscast is a tape-delayed telecast, which would allow for postproduction work to correct any production problems.

Newscast Production Period The production period refers to the inclusive dates (e.g., fiscal year) of newscast production for which the budget is being constructed.

No. of Newscasts The number of individual newscasts budgeted for during this production period is entered here.

Summary of Production Costs This summary area brings forward the subtotals of costs from the respective sections within the budget form. Note that each item in lines 1 through 17 is found as a section head within the budget form. When each section is completed, the section subtotal is listed in this summary table.

Contingency This term refers to the practice of adding a percentage to the subtotal of the summary section (i.e., to lines 1 through 17) as a pad against the difference between actual costs and the estimated costs of all line items. The customary contingency percentage is 15%. Multiply the subtotal in line 19 by 0.15 to determine the contingency figure. Enter that result into line 20. The total of lines 19 and 20 becomes the grand total of the budget costs.

Estimated The *estimated* category refers to costs that can only be projected before the production. Rarely are the estimated costs the same as the final costs because of the number of variables that cannot be anticipated. Every attempt should be made to ensure realistic estimated cost figures and the consideration of as many variables as possible. The challenge of preparing an estimated budget is to project as closely as possible to actual costs.

Actual The *actual* category records the costs that are finally incurred for the respective line items during or after production is completed. The actual costs are those costs that will really be paid. The ideal budget seeks to have actual costs come as close as possible—i.e., be at or, preferably, under—to the estimated costs.

Rights and Clearances This section accounts for the costs that might be incurred in obtaining necessary copyright clearances, synchronization rights, and trademark registration for music and newscast title and logo.

Producing Staff This section accounts for the producing staff and other personnel that may be involved in producing responsibilities. The personnel roles are divided into the three areas of a production: preproduction, production, and postproduction.

Director and Staff This section covers the studio director and personnel associated with the directing responsibilities. As with most budgets, some line items (e.g., secretary) are listed for purposes of suggesting staff members and additional roles that might be needed during large operation newscast production.

Talent The expenses of any on-air talent are accounted for in this section. Some talent may be hired by contract and may be subject to other fees. Other talent may be freelancers.

Benefits Depending on the arrangements made with talent, some production budgets may have to account for benefits accruing to talent and crew members (e.g., health benefits or pensions). Insurance coverage and state and federal taxes that are due to any salaries to talent and crew members should be accounted for in this section.

Production Facility This section lists production facility space that may be required. For each facility space, the technical hardware that may or may not be needed is also listed for consideration. Rate cards for production facilities provide cost information for these spaces and for the technical hardware in them. The executive producer will have to choose what is needed and the projected cost of each item.

Production Staff This section accounts for production staff and crew members for each stage of the production: preproduction, production, and postproduction.

Cameras, Videotape Recording, and Video Engineering Those personnel and expenses associated with the maintenance and use of the video camera are accounted for in this section. This section records the equipment that will need to be purchased or rented. Camera equipment rental will be necessary if any exterior stock shots have to be made.

News Gathering Sources, Materials This section of the budget accounts for the news sources necessary to cover the news. Print, video, and audio sources are listed. Electronic news gathering sources are also suggested.

Electronic News Gathering, Expenses A substantial portion of television news production involves remote news gathering called *electronic news gathering* (ENG). The costs (personnel, hardware, and vehicular) involved in that form of news production are suggested here.

News Set Design, Construction, Decoration, and Properties Studio newscast production will involve the use of a studio set. Consideration has to be made for news set design, construction, decoration, and the properties involved in dressing a news set (e.g., furniture). This section of the budget suggests some design and construction personnel and some construction and property acquisition costs.

Set Lighting The need to create a lighting design for the set requires personnel and equipment for set lighting. Studio costs can be incurred with the use of lighting instruments. The lighting instruments necessary to light the set must be listed in the budget.

Audio Production Audio production and recording are essential to newscast production. This section suggests personnel, hardware, microphones, and the need for equipment rental and purchase line items for the production.

Wardrobe, Make-up, and Hairstyling Regular news production requires clothing changes for talent. The personnel, materials, construction, and care of talent wardrobe are accounted for in this section. Make-up and hairstyling are also necessary to newscast production. This section of the budget suggests some line items to be accounted for regarding make-up, hairstyling, and supplies.

Videotape Stock, Film Stock, and Processing The provision of necessary videotape stock in required sizes, film, and film processing are accounted for in this section. Production of graphics may involve the use of 35mm film and processing. The producer has to consider still photography involving the newscast and the talent as part of newscast production.

Postproduction Editing The personnel, facilities, and materials for postproduction needs during editing are accounted for in this section.

Music Most newscast production will involve original or recorded music. This section of the budget suggests some of the potential costs and personnel involved in the music.

• **Newscast Format Form**

Production process Newscast preproduction

Responsibility News director

Purpose To create the form or design of the newscast or a skeleton for an individual newscast. The format reflects the newscast design and is the result of the design. The format also serves as the rundown sheet critical to the studio production crew during production.

Objective Every news item for a newscast—whether a reader, a video story, or a video package—is placed in its corresponding order in the newscast on the format sheet. This format sheet is identical to the newsroom wall board that serves to construct the individual newscast throughout the news day. The format sheet is broken into the segments of the newscast separated by commercial breaks.

Glossary

Newscast Segment A newscast segment is one of a number of individual units of the newscast each separated by a commercial break.

Story Slug A story slug is an identifier label of a word or two for each news story. A slug identifier also serves to label video packages.

Time The time column records the segment time for each news story or video package.

VID The VID (videotape) column and checklist boxes indicate whether the corresponding story has videotape as part of the story.

GPH The GPH (graphic) column and checklist boxes indicate that the corresponding news story requires a graphic matte as part of the story.

Audio The audio column consists of three choices and three columns of checklist boxes. The audio column indicates the form of audio source corresponding to each story.

vo/crt/lve The choices of audio source origination are voice-over, cartridge, or live. Voice-over means the audio is wedded to the videotape source, crt means the audio source is a prerecorded audio cartridge that must be controlled by the audio director, and lve means the audio source is live in the studio (e.g., the talent) and is picked up by microphones. If the news story begins with a reader from studio talent and continues with voice-over video, then the lve column is checked as well as the vo column. The lve column can be marked with a number 1 to indicate the first audio source as the newscast comes to that story and the vo column marked with a 2 to indicate that the second audio source for that story is the voice-over videotape.

Running/Back Time The final columns in the format sheet record both the running and back times for the newscast. This entry is the sum of the segment times already listed in the time column. Running time begins with 00:00 time and runs to the length (e.g., 28:30) of the newscast. The back time column begins with the total time of the newscast (e.g., 28:30) and all segments of a newscast are subtracted until the end time is 00:00. Note that for both times, the length of the commercial breaks is figured in as part of the calculations.

• **Newscast Design Form**

Production process   Newscast preproduction

Responsibility   News director

Purpose   To design the flow of both video and audio sources to be achieved as part of the production values chosen for the newscast.

Objective   The newscast design form organizes the proposed newscast into individual video change units indicated by the aspect ratio frames down the middle of the form. The news director chooses video elements of each change of video images from the opening to the close of the newscast and assigns corresponding audio sources. Production value choices to be considered include whatever the budget can allow—from the very simple (e.g., coming up live in the studio on anchors and going immediately into news) to the more expensive and sophisticated (e.g., computer designed and animated graphics opening with "bells and whistles").

Glossary

News Director   The news director, whose name is entered here, has the primary responsibility for designing the production values for a newscast.

Executive Producer   The executive producer's name is entered here. The executive producer has a consulting role or has approval responsibility for the final newscast design.

News Producer   The news producer's name is entered here. The news producer plays a consulting role in the design of the newscast and gives approval to the final design.

Newscast Title   After the set and newscast are designed, each newscast has its own title to distinguish one daily newscast from another.

Video Choices   The video choices column allows for the choice of any video source production value designed for any particular aspect ratio frame.

Storyboard   The storyboard column consists of aspect ratio frames for sketching whatever video images make up the video production values for that screen.

Audio Copy   The audio copy column allows the opportunity to note any audio sources chosen to complement the video for each screen frame.

Segment 1   This form is broken into the newscast segments, each separated usually by commercial breaks.

Time   The time column allows the assignment of seconds and minutes to the duration of the video and audio production values chosen. The segment times can be summed up to afford some gauge of the time into the program at any storyboard frame and production value.

• **News Set Design Form**

Production process   Newscast preproduction

Responsibility   News director

Purpose   To design the set for the newscast.

Objective   The news set design form allows for the design of both a bird's eye view and a front view of a proposed studio set. A 17 × 23 unit grid for a bird's eye view allows the assignment of any number of footage per unit to create a set design. The front view allows a 10 × 23 unit grid for design.

Glossary

News Director   The news director's name is entered here. The news director is in charge of and responsible for the design or approval of any final design.

Executive Producer   The name of the executive producer is entered here. The executive producer either is a consultant or, at the news director's discretion, may be involved in the process of designing the set and approving the design.

News Producer   The news producer, whose name is entered here, will play a consulting role or will approve a set design.

Date   The date of the set design creation is entered here.

Newscast: Morning/Noon/Early/Evening/Late   The choice of one of many newscasts indicates that it is conceivable that different daily newscasts might have different sets. The morning newscast would be that newscast aired in the morning; the noon newscast at noon; the early newscast at a late afternoon time slot (e.g., 5:00 PM); the evening newscast at 6:00 PM, usually before a network newscast; and the late newscast at the late evening time slot (e.g., 10:00 PM or 11:00 PM).

Bird's Eye View   The bird's eye view grid is an area for set design from the top looking down. The 17 × 23 units allow the assignment of some uniform unit of measure to each unit of the grid (e.g., one square = 1 foot creates a 23-foot wide set design area; one square = 2 feet creates a 46-foot wide set design area). Width and depth of a proposed set should be indicated on the grid.

Front View   The front view grid is an area for a set design from the front looking straight toward the set. The 10 × 23 units allow the assignment of some uniform measure to each unit of the grid (e.g., one square = 1 foot).

• **Studio Camera Blocking Plot Form**

Production process   Newscast preproduction

Responsibility   Studio director

Purpose   To create the design for the studio cameras from which the studio director will list camera shots, the lighting director will design the lighting plot, and the audio director will design the audio plot for the program.

Objective The camera blocking plot is a preproduction stage preparing the studio director for all details for directing the newscast. From the approved set design and properties list the studio director can design all production elements for news production videotaping.

The studio camera blocking plot records the blocking of talent, cameras, and set properties.

Notes on the creation of the studio camera blocking plot form The studio director should sketch the bird's eye view of the set from the news set design form and properties list. The studio director should then position the talent in the floor plan and indicate the blocking placement or movement of the talent. The studio cameras should be sketched into place to achieve the shot(s) as proposed in the newscast design form and the newscast format form.

Glossary

Director The studio director's name is entered here.

Date The date that the camera blocking form is done is noted here.

Newscast The title of the newscast is recorded here to distinguish this blocking plot from those of other newscasts of the organization.

Set The name or label of the set being blocked is entered here.

Lighting The studio director lists the general lighting needs for the set in this column (e.g., special logo lighting, a chromakey panel, or a live interview area).

Audio The general sound pick-up requirement is recorded here.

Bird's Eye Floor Plan This space is the area in which the bird's eye view of the set is sketched from the set design form for blocking purposes.

Cameras/Properties/Blocking These are the elements to be entered on the bird's eye view of the set. Cameras have to be placed as they are part of blocking, set properties (e.g., furniture) are important to the set, and the placement and movement of talent must be sketched.

Description This block records any verbal description of the action of the program. Some blocking may be better described in words than can be shown in the sketch.

Cameras/Movement/Properties These are the elements of the blocked set that are to be included in any description of the newscast being blocked.

In-cue/Dialogue/Action The in-cue is the dialogue or action prompt that begins some element of the newscast (e.g., talent movement).

Out-cue/Dialogue/Action The out-cue is the dialogue or action prompt on which some newscast element ends.

Comments This section provides more space in which the director can make additional notes on the blocking. All thoughts should be jotted down during preproduction lest they be glossed over or forgotten during production meetings.

• **Studio Camera Shot List Form**

Production process Newscast preproduction

Responsibility Studio director

Purpose To translate the proposed studio camera blocking into studio camera shot lists for each camera.

Objective The shot list form organizes the proposed studio camera blocking on the studio director's studio camera blocking plot into shots listed by studio cameras. Each shot should generate the necessary video to create the proposed edits as designed on the newscast design form and newscast format form. The shot list form will translate each proposed shot from the newscast design form and the newscast format form to individual lists for the camera operators.

Glossary

Camera Operator The name of the camera operator (each of the three) is entered on this line.

Camera: C1/C2/C3 The camera assigned to each camera operator is indicated here by circling the appropriate camera number.

Newscast The title of the newscast is listed here.

Newscast Production Date The date of the newscast production scheduled for the listed camera shots is entered here. Camera shots may be newscast specific (i.e., for one-time use only).

Set The newscast set being used for the listed camera shots is recorded here.

Shot No. Every proposed shot needed to create the generalized camera shots for the newscast should be numbered consecutively on the shot list. The shot numbers are camera specific. The studio director separates the numbered shots and lists them for the individual camera in consecutive order. Each camera shot list will contain the numbered shots assigned to that camera. Those numbers are listed in this column.

Camera Framing Camera framing directions for each proposed shot should use the abbreviations for the basic camera shot framing: XLS, LS, MS, CU, or XCU. This will communicate to the camera operator the lens framing for the proposed shot.

Talent The content of each framed shot is indicated here. The studio director indicates who or what is framed for each defined shot. The object of framing can be the program talent, the news maker, the interviewee, all persons on the set, or a logo.

Camera Movement Camera movement directions indicate the kind of camera movement needed to achieve the proposed shot. Camera movement in a shot may be primary movement. *Primary movement* is movement on the part of the talent in front of the camera. Primary movement will require camera movement—pan, tilt, or pedestal—to follow the talent. Camera movement could be *secondary movement,* which is the movement of the camera itself. This camera movement could also be a dolly, truck, pedestal, or zoom. The studio director should translate those directions to this column for the camera operator.

Special Instructions The studio director may indicate some special instructions for a particular shot or camera operator. Those instructions should be written here. The camera shot list is camera specific, so an individual camera operator can be addressed in these special instructions.

● **News Set Audio Plot Form**

Production process Newscast preproduction

Responsibility Audio director

Purpose To facilitate and encourage the design of sound perspective and audio recording on the set.

Objective The news set audio plot form is designed to prompt the audio director to weigh the set environment and sound production values in planning for audio equipment and quality microphone pick-up and audio recording during production. The audio plot form is intended to encourage preproduction by the audio director.

Glossary

Audio Director The name of the audio director is placed here.
Director/Approval The audio director is required to get the approval of the studio director for the audio plot. The studio director's approval authorizes any expenses incurred for audio coverage of the production.
Newscast Title The title of the news program is listed here.
Date The date the audio plot was designed is entered here.
Set The set for which the audio plot is designed is noted here.
Microphone: Directional/Wireless/Lavaliere/Other The audio director chooses the kinds of microphones to be used.
Microphone Support The audio director weighs and indicates any proposed microphone supports for sound coverage during production.
Sound Effects: Foldback/Other The audio director indicates here what sound effects (e.g., studio foldback) are required. Foldback is necessary for the script prompter to be able to hear the talent reading the script.
Bird's Eye Floor Plan The best preproduction information for the audio director is the floor plan for the set with talent and talent movement indicated. This should be sketched in this box from the camera blocking form. Knowing where the cameras are placed, sound design, and microphone placement is important to the audio director.
Description Any studio director's notes on the elements of the production that will affect sound design and recording should be noted here. For example, excessive movement of talent could affect sound recording and audio control. The fact that some sound foldback is required during the newscast should be noted here.
In-cue In-cues, either visual imaging or audio cues (e.g.,

an opening or closing or bumpers before commercial breaks), should be noted here.

Out-cue The out-cue or final words of audio or visual imaging can affect sound design. Notation of those cues (e.g., an opening or closing or bumpers) should be made here.

● **News Set Lighting Plot Form**

Production process Newscast preproduction

Responsibility Lighting director

Purpose To create and organize the lighting design of the set.

Objective The lighting plot form is designed to facilitate the creation of the lighting design for the lighting director. The plot serves to preplan the placement of lighting instruments, kind of lighting, lighting control, and lighting design. When lighting is preplanned, lighting equipment needs are easily realized and provided.

Notes on the use of the lighting plot form The lighting plot form encourages preplanning for lighting design and production. Hence, the more lighting needs and aesthetics that can be anticipated, the better the lighting production tasks. At a minimum, the lighting design should be created in advance of production. Lighting design can begin as soon as the set construction is complete. The essentials to planning lighting design are the bird's eye floor plan and the talent blocking area of the set. This information is available from the news director's set design form and the camera blocking plot.

Glossary

Lighting Director The name of the lighting director is entered here.
Director/Approval The lighting plot will have to be approved by the studio director. The studio director signs or initials approval on this form. Approval by the studio director authorizes expenses in lighting needs acquisition.
Newscast The newscast for which the set is being lighted is entered here. A news organization may have more than one set, or may light a set differently for the different daily newscasts.
Set The lighting director indicates the name or label for the set being lighted.
Date The date of the design of the lighting plot is entered here.
Lighting This area of the plot notes any basic needs in lighting design (e.g., special logo lighting or chromakey area).
Light Change: Yes/No It is important to lighting design and lighting control to know if the newscast format or the studio director plans any change of lighting during videotaping. This notation alerts the lighting director to that need.
Bird's Eye Floor Plan The best preproduction information for the lighting director is the floor plan for the set with talent blocking and movement area noted and camera placement indicated. These should be sketched

in this box from the studio director's camera blocking plot form. Where the cameras are to be placed is important to the lighting design.

Description   Any studio director's notes on the elements of the production that will affect lighting design should be noted here.

Lighting Instruments/Lighting Accessories/Filters/Newscast Logo/Other Requirements   These lists are designed to assist the lighting director in considering all elements of lighting design and materials or situations in the preparation of the lighting plot. The lighting director can make notes in the proper spaces within each of these categories in planning for the particular design of the news set.

In-cue   The lighting director notes any in-cues from the format form indicating when—i.e., on what visual imaging or audio cue—the lighting design is to begin or change.

Out-cue   The notation of an out-cue of image change or audio cue for the end of a shot or a change of lighting is recorded here.

- **Talent Audition Form**

Production process   Newscast preproduction

Responsibility   News director

Purpose   To gather and record relevant information at the time of talent auditions on the background and professional experience of prospective anchors, co-anchors, weathercasters, sportscasters, editorialists, feature producers, or reporters/writers.

Objective   The talent audition form is filled out by the prospective talent who wishes to audition for the role of an anchor, co-anchor, weathercaster, sportscaster, editorialist, feature producer, or reporter/writer. The form gathers pertinent information that will allow the news director to make an enlightened choice for talent given an audition videotape and this form.

Glossary

News Director   The name of the news director responsible for the development of the newscast is entered here.

Newscast   The title of the newscast is recorded here.

Position: Anchor/Weathercaster/Sportscaster/Feature Producer/Reporter/Writer   The prospective talent chooses the role for which to audition by checking the applicable box(es).

Name/etc.   This area of personal demographic information is standard background data for each applicant.

Availability   This area of the form screens for prospective talent availability for further in-studio auditions and production taping sessions. Previous commitments may have to be altered based on this information.

Personal Data   This area of the form gathers information that goes on file for the news director as data that may become relevant when wardrobe trades, for example, become available to the talent.

Agent/Union Affiliations   It is important for the news director to know to what union or professional guilds

a prospective talent belongs. This information may be necessary when payment of fees to those organizations become due.

Questions   These three questions give the producer some open-ended information from prospective talent on interest in the news program, past experience, and qualifications.

The application informs the applicant that a résumé or list of previous experience in related media and a still photo are expected.

- **News Beat/Future File Form**

Production process   Newscast preproduction

Responsibility   Reporter/Writer or Feature Producer

Purpose   To structure the assignment and the monitoring of the news beats for which each reporter/writer or feature producer is responsible. The news beats also serve as future files or resource databases for potential or future news makers.

Objective   The news beat/future file form helps the reporter/writer and feature producer organize and report information about an assigned news beat. The news beat/future file also facilitates gathering similar information for entry into computer databases in the newsroom.

Glossary

Compiler   The compiler is the reporter/writer or feature producer to whom the news director assigns the particular beat or future file.

Source   The source catalogs any primary or single resource for the information contained on the form. If there is no one single resource, the compiler indicates "many."

Organization Title/Beat   This category records the title of the organization being researched or the title of the assigned beat.

General Offices/Address   The mailing address of the organization listed above or a contact address for the news beat news maker is entered here.

Telephone No.   Record the main telephone number of the organization or news beat.

Public Relations Officer   Listing a contact person, such as the public relations officer, is important to developing good beat relationships. The contact person's phone number and personal extension aids in contacting the beat news maker.

Press Officer   Listing a press officer for the organization or news beat facilitates swift contact for reaction to news from a spokesperson for the organization or news beat news maker.

Communication Office   Having a communication office similar to an information office for the purpose of communicating to the press also facilitates contact and reaction from an organization or news beat news maker.

Organizational Goals/Objectives   This area of the form encourages some statement from the compiler summarizing the background and place of the organization or news beat in the area of news gathering.

On File   The on file section allows the compiler to

indicate what in-house resources are available on the organization or news beat. On file has some options that are most common and space to indicate other choices.

Entered into Database This space allows the compiler to log when the information was entered into a computer database and when the information was updated.

• **Newscast Assignment Form**

Production process Newscast preproduction

Responsibility Assignment editor and/or feature producer

Purpose To assign reporters/writers and feature producers to news stories or feature packages. The assignment forms are distributed before, during, or after the daily newscast planning conference. A feature producer wishing to propose a feature package uses this form.

Objective The newscast assignment form organizes and details a news story or feature package topic that facilitates getting started on a story for a reporter/writer and beginning a feature package for a feature producer. The assignment form also serves to assign a videographer to the reporter/writer or feature producer. A feature producer uses this form to propose a feature package to the assignment editor.

Glossary

Reporter/Feature Producer The name of the reporter or feature producer is listed at the top of the form.

Videographer The assignment editor uses the newscast assignment form to assign a videographer to a reporter or feature producer.

Today's Date The current date is entered here.

Newscast Date This entry assigns a newscast date to the reporter or feature producer.

Story Assignment A check in this box indicates that the following information is a clear assignment.

Deadline If the story assignment box is checked, a deadline date should also be entered.

Air Date When the assignment is a story assignment and a deadline is given, a newscast air date should also be given.

Proposal Placing a check in the proposal box indicates that the assignment editor is simply proposing an idea for a news story or feature package and not assigning it. A feature producer checks this category if this form is being used as a proposal for a feature producer.

Approved A check or initials in the approval category indicates that the proposal was approved and the reporter/writer or feature producer can begin the project.

Recommendation Only This category allows an assignment editor to recommend an idea to a reporter or feature producer.

FYI FYI means "for your information." The assignment editor may just be passing some idea or information along to a reporter or feature producer.

Initiative This category means that the assignment ed-

itor recommends an idea for the initiative of the reporter/ writer or feature producer and sees no commitment unless the reporter or feature producer moves on the idea.

Personal Interest This entry means that the attached information or idea is for the reporter or feature producer's own personal interest only. The assignment editor may know that the reporter or feature producer has some interest in the idea or is already working on the topic, and this adds some new information.

News Story If this unit of the form is completed, the assignment is a news story usually intended for the newscast of the day.

News Slug For purposes of indicating the story on the format board and format/rundown sheet, the story is slugged from the moment of assignment with a word or two identifier.

Event This entry describes the news event to be covered. It could be a person or a thing.

Date/Time/Place These entries give essential information to the reporter or feature producer to plan on covering the news event listed above.

Travel Directions If the assigned news event is not very close, travel directions can be included for the convenience of the reporter/writer or feature producer.

Story Description A brief description of the news story will help the reporter/writer or feature producer get oriented swiftly to covering the event.

Background The assignment editor can give some background information to the news story or event, which will provide the reporter/writer or feature producer some leads to covering the story.

Contact Person Some news stories may have come from leads telephoned or mailed in to the newsroom. Others may have come from a contact that older reporters and assignment editors have gained through experience.

Phone If the contact person telephoned in the lead, a telephone number is a helpful lead to a reporter/writer or feature producer.

Additional Leads Besides basic information and background, there are other leads a reporter or feature producer could use to get to a story or news maker, and these leads should be listed here.

Feature Package Another option for an assignment editor is to assign a feature package to a feature producer. This unit of the form is used for a feature package assignment.

Title Feature packages are routinely given a working title by which they will be referred.

Unit This category indicates whether the assignment is for a single unit package.

Series This category is used to indicate that the feature package is a series. The number of expected units in a series can be indicated below.

Idea Most feature packages begin with an idea. The idea is stated in this entry.

Objective(s) A feature producer should not begin a video project without knowing or setting goals or objectives.

Location(s) The assignment editor may suggest remote

locations for videotaping the feature package. If the feature producer is using this form to propose a package, suggested location(s) are entered here.

Contact(s) The assignment editor may have some contact person(s) who can aid in the production of the feature package. Or, a producer writing this as a proposal can indicate the contact people for the package. A phone number is presented as a lead to the contact person.

Background/Leads The assignment editor may have other background information to offer to a feature producer, or the feature producer proposing the feature package may indicate additional background to the idea as well as other leads.

See Attached When the assigning editor or proposing producer has some attached copy, notation to that effect should be made here.

Let's Meet on This If either the assignment editor or feature producer of a proposal would like to have a conference on the idea, notation should be made here. Either party should move to set an appointment with the other.

- **Graphic Design Request Form**

Production process Newscast preproduction

Responsibility News producer, graphic artist/producer, reporters/writers

Purpose To record those graphics needed as a video matte source or full screen source during production, usually to complement a news story or video package.

Objective The graphic design request form allows the news producer to request a graphic for each news story. The graphic artist/producer may also be a part of creating the requests for graphics, working from the assigned stories. The reporters/writers and feature producer also make graphic design requests after writing their stories.

Glossary

News Producer Because the news producer oversees producing the news stories, the news producer is closest to the stories and to the graphics requirements for each story. The name of the news producer requesting graphics is entered here.

Reporter/Writer The name of the reporter/writer who is requesting graphics is logged here.

Feature Producer The name of the feature producer requesting graphics is entered on this line.

Graphic Artist/Producer The graphic artist/producer for the newscast is listed here.

Date Requested The date on which the graphic design request was made is entered here.

Newscast The choice of newscast within a news organization is important with regard to the assignment. The timing of the production of the graphics depends on whether the graphics requests were made for the morning, noon, early, evening, or late newscast.

Deadline The assignment editor, reporter, or feature producer sets a deadline date and time for the completion of the graphics. It is conceivable that some graphics requested could be for a future newscast and not just for the daily newscast.

Graphic No. In this column the graphics being requested can be numbered consecutively for purposes of calculating the total number of graphics being requested or for showing the order in which each graphic is to be inserted into the newscast.

Story Slug/Feature Title This box permits the news producer, reporter, or feature producer to give the graphic artist/producer an identifier in the way of a story slug (a word or two of the title of a feature package) to help in creating or selecting the imaging for the graphic.

Notes: Content Description This box permits the news producer, reporter, or feature producer the opportunity to describe the content of the news story or feature package as a gauge of a graphic's image or to provide a description of a graphic to be created.

Status This column allows the graphic artist/producer to record the current status of the requested graphic: available already (perhaps created and used previously), unavailable or not to be used again, or needing to be designed and produced.

- **Emergency Services Call Log Form**

Production process Newscast preproduction

Responsibility Assignment editor

Purpose To track the daily telephone calls to all emergency services in the newscast reporting area.

Objective The emergency services call log provides the necessary weekly breakdown of all emergency service units for each municipality within the telecast market.

Glossary

Assignment Editor The assignment editor is responsible for monitoring all news generating sources. Emergency services (e.g., police, fire, and hospitals) are a primary source of breaking news and news follow-up within a telecast area. The name of the assignment editor is recorded here.

Week of The date of the week of the record contained on the log is entered here.

Municipality There are a number of municipalities within any telecast area (e.g., city, town, or village). The names of the different municipalities to be covered are entered here.

Fire The name of the fire department of each municipality is recorded here.

Police: City/County/State Insofar as there are many levels of police within any telecast area, the various police departments are listed.

Hospital Hospitals are the sources for breaking news of emergencies. The name(s) of the local hospital(s) are listed here.

Code/Prefix/Number For each emergency recorded, the

corresponding emergency code can be listed (where codes exist) or the applicable telephone number can be entered.

Days of the Week Columns of checklist boxes are used to log the calls as they are made to each emergency service listed.

• **Remote Assignment Form**

Production process Newscast preproduction

Responsibility Assignment editor, news producer

Purpose To track the travel and destination of reporters, feature producers, and videographers as well as the use of camera equipment and news vehicles in news gathering preparation.

Objective The remote assignment form is a hand copy of the remote assignment board in the newsroom. The form keeps track of video stories or feature packages; the reporters and feature producers; the assigned videographers and video camera equipment; and the reservation, destination, and departure and return times of the news vehicles. This form also alerts the news producer to available personnel given the newsroom return entries.

Glossary

Assignment Editor The assignment editor assigns video stories to reporters and videographers. The name of the assignment editor is recorded here.

News Producer The news producer monitors and makes other assignments of videographers, so needs to know where personnel and news stories are during the day. The name of the news producer is entered here.

Newscast The name of the newscast within the news organization to which the video assignment pertains is recorded here.

Date The date of the newscast preparation day is entered here.

Story/Feature The slug describing the news story or the title of the feature package is entered here.

Reporter/Producer The name of the reporter or feature producer responsible for the video story or video package is recorded here.

Videographer The name of the videographer responsible for videotaping the project is recorded here.

Camera Unit The number or name of the video camera equipment unit being reserved or used is entered here.

Vehicle The name or number of the news vehicle being reserved or used is recorded here.

Destination The location of remote videotaping is recorded here.

Depart: AM/PM The newsroom departure time is recorded here, with the correct time of day circled.

Return: AM/PM When the crew returns, the time of return from location videotaping is entered here, with the correct time of day circled.

• **Editor/Editing Reservation Form**

Production process Newscast preproduction

Responsibility Assignment editor, news producer

Purpose To track the reservation and use of the videotape editing suites for videotape editing by the reporter/writer or feature producer and video editor.

Objective The editor/editing reservation form is a hand copy of the video editor/editing suite reservation board in the newsroom. This form keeps track of editing suite reservation times by news story or feature package and by reporter/writer or feature producer and video editor.

Glossary

Assignment Editor The assignment editor makes the first assignment of video editors to reporters/writers and feature producers. The name of the assignment editor is entered here.

News Producer The news producer is responsible for personnel and equipment and for getting the newscast produced. The news producer oversees the reservation and use of editing suites and video editors. The name of the news producer is entered here.

Newscast The newscast for which the videotape editing is scheduled is entered here.

Date The news preparation day for which editing reservations are logged is entered here.

Story/Feature This column records the slug or title of the video editing project being logged.

Reporter/Producer The reporter/writer or feature producer whose video editing project is being logged is recorded here.

Video Editor The video editor assigned to do the editing for the project being logged is recorded here.

Editing Suite The name, label, or number of video editing suites available for videotape editing is logged here.

Special Effects Any special effects required by the video being edited (e.g., control room access or digital video effects hardware) are recorded here.

Special Instructions This space allows for any additional information on video editing project of interest to any personnel involved.

Begin Session: AM/PM The beginning time of the editing suite reservation is entered here, with the correct time of day circled.

End Session: AM/PM The expected end of the editing suite reservation is entered here, with the correct time of day circled.

• **Video Production Calendar Form**

Production process Newscast preproduction

Responsibility News producer

Purpose To track the production of all feature packages from assignment stage to deadline and completion.

Objective The video production calendar is a hand form similar to the video production calendar board in the newsroom. This form facilitates tracking the production of all feature packages for the news director. This form tracks each feature package by feature producer, by stages of production, and by a day-by-day monthly calendar.

Glossary

News Producer The name of the news producer responsible for the feature packages is entered here.

Newscast If there is more than one newscast being produced by the news organization, the name of the newscast for which the feature packages are being produced is listed here.

Producer The name of the feature producer assigned a feature package is entered here.

Videographer The videographer assigned to the feature producer for a particular project is entered here.

Video Editor The video editor assigned to the project is entered here.

Assign. This column records the date that the feature package was assigned to the feature producer.

Treatment This column records the date that the treatment for the feature package was approved.

Preproduction Script This column records the date that the preproduction script was completed and approved (if required).

Location The field location at which the feature package video will be shot is recorded here.

Shooting Schedule The date(s) when the location video for the feature package is scheduled to be shot is recorded here.

Editing Date This column records the editing suite reservation date(s) when the feature package video is scheduled to be edited.

Deadline This column records the deadline or airing date for the feature package.

Calendar The blank calendar encourages the news producer to track the day-to-day progress of each assigned feature package. This can be accomplished by using a different color pen for each feature producer or package.

Notes This area of the form allows the news producer additional space to make notes about the feature producers and their feature packages.

• Package Treatment Form

Production process Newscast preproduction

Responsibility Feature producer

Purpose To propose a feature package to the assignment editor, news producer, or news director.

Objective The package treatment form attempts to focus elements of the proposed feature package for the feature producer as a step to presenting the idea or concept to newscast personnel for approval. The basic requirements in order for the newscast personnel to judge the appropriateness of the video package include goals and objectives for the feature package and some verbal description of the proposed visual imaging.

Glossary

Feature Producer The name of the reporter/writer or feature producer who is proposing the package treatment is entered here.

Videographer The proposed videographer's name is entered here.

Date The date that the proposal was completed should be entered here.

Location(s) The remote location(s) that may involve travel for the producer and videographer should be noted here.

Proposed Title A working title is appropriate to the proposed feature package described in the treatment. There is an advantage to titling a proposed feature package: In the synthesis of a simple title can be contained a concept or idea that paragraphs cannot convey.

Proposed Length Committing to a time length for the feature package is a good discipline for the feature producer. In many news production operations, all video packages will have to fall within a given time length. The time length commitment gives management personnel an idea of the likelihood of the success of the feature package and its content in terms of its length.

Proposed Shooting Date Assignment editors and news producers have to operate in terms of a calendar of feature packages for the newscast. The commitment to a shooting date allows more information into the approval process.

Proposed Completion Date Another bit of information for an assignment editor or news producer is the estimated date for the completion of the feature package. Completion dates will depend on the content and challenge of videotaping a topic and editing the source tapes.

Production Statement A production statement is a very brief emotional or rational verbal expression that will serve as a reminder throughout the feature package's production of the specific goal or objective of the package. The production statement is meant to be a constant reminder to the feature producer of the precise goal of the message of the feature package. An example of a production statement for a video package on senior citizen exercise groups is, "Being senior is being strong."

Communication Goals and Objectives of the Package Communication goals and objectives of the proposed feature package should contain the rationale for doing the proposed package, a description of the target audience, the audience need for the package in terms of the topic, and the interest in the topic on the part of the audience. The more information that can be given in this section of the treatment aids the assignment editor or news producer in judging the suitability of the proposed feature package.

Package Treatment The treatment itself is the verbal description of the proposed feature package, including proposed interviewees, questions for the interview, proposed cutaways for the piece, and shooting locations. The more information that is available at this stage of preproduction the better an assignment editor or news producer can judge the treatment for approval.

The package treatment should be seen as a synopsis of the proposed feature package. It might also include about five of the most important questions to be answered in the feature package. Story elements to be established at the beginning, in the middle, and at the end of the proposed package should be addressed.

• **Television Script Form**

Production process Newscast preproduction, feature package postproduction

Responsibility Reporter/writer, feature producer

Purpose To coordinate in side-by-side columns audio copy and a verbal description of the video imaging of the feature package.

Objective As a preproduction script, the proposed audio copy and the verbal description of the proposed feature package can be expressed in acceptable script form. It is the first format stage in firming up a feature package.

As a final production script in postproduction, the two column format coordinates the final draft of the feature package drawn from the preproduction script and the editing work sheet of the source tapes.

Glossary

Feature Producer The name of the producer of the feature package is entered here.

Videographer The name of the assigned or proposed videographer is entered here.

Package Title The title of the feature package as it will be known is recorded here.

Length For the preproduction script, the entry for the length of the proposed feature package is an estimate.
For the final production script, the entry for the length should be more accurate. It may reflect an assigned length to the feature package.

Video The video column contains an abbreviated verbal description of the video elements of the feature package. This column contains image content descriptions and framing (e.g., XLS of New York City Skyline), editing transitions (e.g., dissolve, cut, or fade), and special effects (e.g., DVE rotation), cut-ins, cut-aways, and character generator copy. For example:

VIDEO

XLS New York City Skyline;
Diss to MS house front;
Cut to CU Mrs. Betty Kasper

Super LT   MRS. BETTY KASPER
                           Artist

Audio The audio column contains the full verbal copy to accompany the video described in the video column. Audio copy is written first in the development of a script. Audio copy should be typed in all caps. All talent and production directions are typed in upper and lower case. All audio copy should be introduced with the label of the talent intended to deliver the copy. The audio column also records the use of sound effects, music, and ambience.

In the preproduction script, proposed interview questions should be included.
In a final production script, audio bites from source tapes should be transcribed and included in the audio column. For example:

AUDIO

SFX: City street traffic sounds.
ANN: NOT EVERYONE LIVING IN NEW YORK CITY SUFFERS FROM THE IMPERSONALIZATION OF THE BIG APPLE.

• **Video Script/Storyboard Form**

Production process Newscast preproduction, feature package postproduction

Responsibility Feature producer

Purpose To coordinate a verbal description of the feature package and the proposed audio copy with corresponding storyboard frames.

Objective The video script and storyboard combination form is an alternative script form in which each corresponding storyboard frame is coordinated with the verbal visual description and audio copy.

Glossary

Feature Producer The name of the producer for the feature package is entered here.

Videographer The assigned or proposed videographer's name is entered here.

Package Title Once a title has been agreed upon, usually from an approved proposal stage, the title should be indicated whenever reference to the feature package is made.

Package Length The proposed length of the feature package is noted in this space.

Date The current date should be entered here.

Video This column contains a simplified verbal description of the video content, camera framing, edit transition, and character generator copy of the proposed feature package.

Storyboard Frame Those storyboard frames are used that coordinate with the entry in the video column. Not all frames will be used or needed. Simply skip those frames that do not match video and audio entries.

Audio This column contains all audio copy for the proposed video package. As with any television script, audio copy should be written first, then the video descriptions opposite the respective audio cue should be created. On this form the storyboard frame is sketched corresponding to the first line of each new video column entry.

• **Graphic Design Form**

Production process Newscast preproduction

Responsibility Feature producer, assignment editor, news producer, reporter/writer, graphic artist/producer

Purpose To create a sketch for a proposed or requested graphic giving the required details and text information for its production.

Objective During preproduction, various producers need to design a news or feature specific graphic or series of graphics for a news story or feature package. This form facilitates the required imaging and text information that may be needed by the graphic artist/producer for production of the graphic(s).

Glossary

News Producer The news producer's name is entered here if the news producer requests or designs the graphic(s).

Assignment Editor The assignment editor's name is entered here if the assignment editor has requested or designed the graphic(s).

Reporter/Writer The name of the reporter/writer is entered here if the reporter/writer is requesting or designing the graphic(s).

Feature Producer The name of the feature producer who requests or designs the graphic(s) is entered here.

Graphic Artist/Producer The name of the graphic artist/producer to whom the design request is submitted is entered here.

Date This is the current date the request for the graphic design is submitted.

Newscast Date This entry indicates the date of the newscast for which the graphic is to be used.

Deadline This is the date when the graphic will have to be completed for insert editing purposes. Completed graphics will require an earlier deadline than that for the news story or feature package. Graphics will have to be completed before videotape editing of the news story or feature package.

Graphic No. This entry assigns a number within the news story or feature package of graphics to be used in the edited video.

Storyboard Frame/Aspect Ratio This storyboard frame gives the person designing the graphic an opportunity to sketch some proposed imaging, paste up a proposed image, or type the required text for the graphic.

Story Slug/Feature Title This information gives the graphic artist/producer a label for the graphic.

Concept The concept permits the person requesting the graphic to supply a verbal description of what is being proposed as imaging information.

Text Many graphics require some text. This is the place to type the required text.

Image Design This area allows the person proposing the graphic design to verbalize the proposed imaging elements.

• **Script Breakdown Form**

Production process Newscast preproduction

Responsibility Feature producer

Purpose To break the preproduction script down into production units usually according to common location or talent requirements.

Objective The script breakdown form organizes the preproduction script from proposed edited order of a final

video to a shooting order according to differing common criteria for the shoots (e.g., location similarity or talent availability). The breakdown form will help organize the shooting units by script pages or number of script lines for managing the remote production.

Glossary

Feature Producer The name of the feature producer is entered here.

Videographer The name of the assigned videographer should be entered here.

Package Title The title of the feature package should be entered here.

Length This entry records the estimated length of the final feature package.

Script Length The length of the preproduction script in number of script pages is recorded here.

Script Pages The number of script pages is one of several modes of measuring the length of a remote shooting unit. This method uses the number of whole or partial pages of script copy as a determinant of the length of a shooting unit.

No. of Script Lines The number of lines of script is another determinant of length of a shooting unit. Every line of talent copy to be recorded during the unit shoot should be counted.

Int/Ext These abbreviations stand for interior/exterior and refer to the script demands for shooting indoors or outdoors. Whether the shoot is an interior or an exterior shoot can also be a determinant for the script breakdown and shooting unit.

Time The time of day or night that the location and interior/exterior setting requires should be recorded here.

Setting Setting means the specific area of a required location (e.g., a setting would be the parents' bedroom for the Smith's home location site).

Location The location column records the remote location at which the setting is to be found (e.g., the Smith's home is the location site for the parents' bedroom).

Talent This entry records by name the specific talent required in the setting at the location for a particular shoot.

Shooting Order When the entire script is broken down into shooting units, the producer can determine the units for individual shoots as well as the consecutive shooting order for the entire remote project.

• **Remote Camera Shot List Form**

Production process Newscast preproduction

Responsibility Feature producer

Purpose To translate the preproduction script from the script breakdown into location shooting units or camera takes.

Objective The remote camera shot list form organizes each proposed videotape take on location into shooting units. The shooting units will generate the necessary video to create the feature package as designed on the preproduction script. This preproduction task facilitates the "what's next" syndrome during location production. The shot list should exactly define each camera set-up, lens framing, and video shot needed.

Glossary

Feature Producer   The name of the feature producer is entered here.

Videographer   The videographer assigned to the feature producer is noted here.

Package Title   The title assigned to the feature package is listed here.

Location   Every planned location site camera set-up and change of location site camera set-up should be noted in this column.

Shot No.   From the script breakdown form, every camera shot needed to create the imaging of the preproduction script should be numbered consecutively. The respective number should be recorded here.

Master Shot   If a proposed shot is a master or establishing shot (e.g., XLS) for a scene it should be noted here. For example, a master shot might be an XLS of a couple walking toward the camera during dialogue.

Cut-in Shot   If a proposed shot is a cut-in (from a master shot) it should be noted in this column. For example, a cut-in would be a CU shot of one of the people in the master shot.

Cut-away Shot   Unlike the cut-in (to a master shot), the cut-away shot is relevant but extraneous to (usually away from) the master scene shot. An example of a cut-away would be generic footage of a city street.

Shot Framing   Shot framing directions for every proposed shot should make use of the symbols for the basic camera shot framing: XLS, LS, MS, CU, and XCU. This would communicate to the camera operator the lens framing for the proposed shot.

Shot Motion   Shot motion directions should indicate the kind of movement desired in the proposed shot. Movement in a shot can be either primary movement (the blocking of the talent; i.e., the talent moves in front of the camera) or secondary movement (the pan, tilt, arc, truck, dolly, pedestal, or zoom; i.e., the camera moves).

Content Notes   Any details of any shot that are not covered in the previous directions can be noted here. An example of a content note would be to direct the camera operator to defocus the lens during the shot.

• Location Site Survey Form

Production process   Newscast preproduction

Responsibility   Feature producer

Purpose   To organize and facilitate the survey of possible remote video production locations for feature package production.

Objective   The location site survey form is designed to assist the feature producer search out and describe potential remote locations for video production purposes. Because many sites may have to be evaluated for a particular

shoot, details of each site will have to be recorded, evaluated, and approved at a later time by the producer and usually away from the site. This form is designed to raise all possible production needs and location details for a successful remote production. The form serves to organize and record location site details for evaluation away from the site.

Glossary

Feature Producer   The name of the feature producer is entered here.

Package Title   The proposed title for the feature package is entered here. At this stage of preproduction, the title may be only a working title.

Date   The date the location survey was made is entered here.

Newscast   The particular newscast for which this feature package is being produced should be entered here (e.g., morning newscast, noon newscast, etc.).

Assigned Deadline   The date for the deadline assigned to the completion of this feature package should be entered here.

Location   The actual location called for in the script should be recorded here. For example, "Bob's bedroom."

Site Identification   This entry should correspond with a city map identification (e.g., H−3) or the name of the location (e.g., Town Point Park).

Local Contact Person   The name of the responsible owner, manager, or supervisory officer of a proposed location should be recorded here. This is the feature producer's contact person at the highest level of authority over a proposed location site. This person has the authority to grant use of the location. The name, title, street address, city, state, and phone number of the contact person should be accurately recorded. All of this information, including the proper title, will be needed for mail correspondence.

Comments   The comments space allows for any notes about the contact person (e.g., executive secretary's name) that would be relevant.

Facilities Personnel   The facilities personnel information is a record of the person with whom the feature producer and production crew will work on location. For example, the maintenance engineer, office manager, and janitor are the individuals responsible for the everyday operation of the proposed location. The name, title, street address, city, state, and phone number are recorded. This information becomes the most practical to the production crew and to the producer. This is the information most used once the location is chosen.

Comments   The comments space is used for any other relevant information about the facilities personnel. For example, the directions to the facilities personnel office at the location or to the maintenance workshop should be recorded here.

Lighting Problems Defined   This area of the form focuses on those details of the proposed location that can affect lighting of the location.

Light Contrast Ratios   The feature producer notes any extreme light areas of the environment. A light meter can read and a record should be made of the extreme lighting intensity of any existing areas of the environment. For example, one end of a proposed location site may have no windows and no ceiling lights. The light reading for this end of the room will be very low to nonexistent, while the other end of the room may be flooded with light from a number of windows. The light reading at this end of the room will be very high. These readings form the contrast ratio between the most existing light and least existing light for the room.

Lighting Intensity   This entry records the highest light level reading in the proposed location. This information will tell the producer that some controls will have to be used on the light source or other light will have to be created to balance this light intensity.

Ceiling Height   The height of an existing ceiling is important to know. For example, ceiling height indicates the available height for lighting stands for lighting instruments that will be used. A low ceiling will allow light to be bounced and a high ceiling means that light will be absorbed, which must be taken into account. High ceilings also demand a lot of light if the ceiling needs to be lit.

Windows/Compass Direction   Knowing the number of windows opening to the exterior of the location is important. Many windows may require correcting incandescent lights with filters or may need to be gelled. Another important fact about a location environment with windows is knowledge of their compass direction. East facing windows get a flood of strong morning sunlight that can increase the lighting intensity in the location environment. West facing windows will create the same problem in the afternoon. When working remote locations, the strongest light source is the sun, which is constantly moving. Knowing the direction of that moving light source is very important. Shadows and reflections change constantly. It is good practice to have a compass when scouting locations and take an accurate reading of due east.

Existing Light Control   A question to ask facilities personnel during location scouting concerns the control of existing lighting. For example, in an all fluorescent lighting environment, there may be one master switch. It would be important to know where it is. Simple wall switches for other light control should also be noted.

Lighting Use   Notation is made of how existing lighting is used. For example, lighted display cases in the environment, parking lot lights, or night lights are conditions of lighting use in the location environment. Much of such light use cannot be controlled.

Floor Description   A description of the type of flooring in a proposed location is entered here. The type of flooring can have consequences for set lighting design. For example, a highly polished floor covering will reflect light and a dark carpet will absorb light or reflect unwanted hues.

Special Consideration   This space is used to record any other specific location details that might affect lighting design in the environment. For example, a pool of water could reflect light as could a mirror on a wall.

Power Problems Defined   This area of the form focuses on and records those details that have to do with electrical power sources. Video production equipment relies heavily on available power sources.

Number of Power Outlets   Count is made of the number of electrical power outlets in the immediate environment of the proposed location. Additional count is made of those outlets that can be accessed by power cable runs.

Number of Separate Circuits   It is important to know how many separate electrical circuits are represented by the power outlets. This is a question for the facilities personnel/maintenance engineer. The power outlets and separate circuits should be noted on a location diagram.

Types of Fuses   One liability of heavy electrical needs for video production equipment is the frequency of blown fuses. In some facilities, restoring power is not just a matter of resetting a circuit but of replacing a fuse. A good example of the need for fuses is in the older private home. Fuses come in many sizes and wattages. It is important to know both size and wattage for the proposed location.

Number of Outlet Prongs   There are two common types of electrical outlets: the two prong and the three prong. Many older environments have only the two-prong outlets. Almost all video production equipment has three-prong plugs. Hence, adapters will have to be used on all two-prong outlets. The number of two-prong outlets will have to be determined during location scouting so adapters can be provided.

Location of Circuit Breakers   Given the common occurrence of overloading circuit breakers with video production equipment, the location of fuse boxes and circuit breakers should be known. Very often, crew members will have to reset breakers and replace blown fuses.

Portable Generator Need   It may happen that there is no power source available in a proposed location. The only possible source of electricity may be a portable power generator. Power generators can be easily rented if needed. Caution must be exercised with the use of a power generator. They are a source of unwanted noise and can be difficult to control.

Audio Problems Defined   This area of the form focuses on details that will affect the production of audio recording in the proposed location environment.

Interior Environmental Sounds   This entry should contain all perceived sound that is audible in the interior of the proposed location. This means careful listening for hums and buzzes from air conditioning, refrigerators, freezers, sound speakers, copying machines, and fluorescent lights. All sounds should be noted. Note should also be made on the ability to control or turn off the sounds.

Ceiling Composition   The composition of a ceiling can determine the quality of sound recordings made in the proposed location. For example, a hard composition ceiling will reflect sound; soundproofing materials on a ceiling will absorb sound. Both can make a difference in the quality of sound recording.

Wall Composition   The composition of the walls at a proposed location environment will also make a difference in the quality of sound recorded in that environment. For example, cork, carpet or cloth, and soundproofing will absorb sound; tile, mirror, and plaster will reflect sound.

Exterior Environmental Sounds The feature producer must listen carefully to both environmental interior and exterior sounds in an environment. Exterior sounds will affect both an exterior and an interior shoot. For example, some common exterior sounds that can affect an interior shoot are airplanes, emergency vehicles, school playground, busy highway, and noisy manufacturing plant. Make a note of every perceivable sound.

Floor Covering Composition The composition of a floor will also have an effect on sound recording. For example, a polished hardwood or tile floor will reflect sound as well as create sound (e.g., footsteps). Deep pile carpeting will absorb sound.

Cast and Crew Needs This area of the form reminds the feature producer that care and consideration of cast and crew needs will have to be accounted for during a location shoot.

Restroom Facilities Restroom facilities for men and women will have to be provided. Part of the location site survey is to note, perhaps on the diagram of the location, the location of the restroom facilities closest to the shooting area.

Green Room Availability A *green room* is a theater term for a waiting area for actors. Such a waiting area may also be required for the talent for a feature package. This should be a room close to but separate from the shooting area, where the talent can relax and await their blocking and videotaping calls.

Parking Arrangements A remote video production crew and talent can create a parking space demand on a neighborhood or public parking area. During scouting, the question of special parking should be addressed. This may occasion some parking privileges or special directions or restrictions.

Freight Elevator In some locations, the number of crew, talent, and equipment involved in video production may require the use of a freight elevator in a facility. The location of the freight elevator should be part of a location environment diagram, giving directions from the freight elevator to the shooting area.

Eating Facilities When the length of a shoot will require a meal on location, some eating facility, special room, or vending machines should be noted. Some facilities may prohibit eating on the premises. Notation then will have to be made of restaurants in the vicinity of the proposed location.

Make-up Facilities If the video production requires that talent appear in make-up, some facility will have to be provided for the application of the make-up. Ideally, make-up application demands mirrors, adequate lighting, and sinks. Restroom facilities make decent make-up preparation accommodations. If nothing else is available, a double set of restrooms can be designated for make-up and dressing.

Loading/Unloading Restrictions The amount of equipment needed for a remote video production may require special loading and unloading arrangements at a location site (e.g., an outside loading dock area). Such an unloading dock may also be close to a freight elevator.

Location personnel should always be made aware of the great amount of equipment video production requires. They should determine any special requirements for so much equipment.

Hardware Store Since remote video production demands much hardware, there is often the need to purchase supplies or replace broken, lost, or forgotten items. Representatives of the facility may know where the closest hardware store is in the vicinity of the proposed location environment.

Civil Emergency Services This area of the form lists essential civil services in the service of the production crew, talent, and location site.

Police Station The address and phone number of the police station that serves the proposed location site is important contact information. The number of individuals in a remote video production crew, the amount of equipment, and the use of an environment warrant the sensitivity to police presence and availability.

Fire Station The same holds true for the fire station within the area of the proposed location. The heavy use of electrical power for a remote video production shoot should alert the producer and the production crew to the potential dangers of the use of so much power. This is especially true for an older facility such as a private home used as a location site. The address and phone number of the fire station should be entered here.

Location Security and Equipment Safety This area of the form records important information on general personnel and property security and safety.

Facility security This entry records the general security of crew, talent, and equipment during the production shoot. Some proposed locations in highly public areas like a shopping mall will present a security risk; confined production sites like a private home would be more secure. Note should be made of apparent security in general for all production elements.

Personnel Valuables Security Record should be made of the arrangements made with facilities personnel for the safety and security of personal belongings—especially of wallets and purses—while the crew and talent are involved in production. Facilities personnel often can provide a locked and secure room for the deposit of personal valuables during production.

Equipment Safe Storage Arrangements should be made for the security of unused equipment and accessories that should be safely stored until needed or stored after use until the location strike. The facilities personnel can often provide a locked and secure room for equipment storage.

Overnight Storage/Security Often remote location shoots will take place over a period of more than one day. This will entail the safe and secure storage of equipment overnight. Complete breakdown of all location equipment and loading, transport, and unloading a second day can result in the loss of valuable time and energy. Facilities personnel can often provide adequate overnight storage that is both safe and secure.

Other Relevant Information This area of the form records other important information that falls outside the other areas of location details.

Public Area Power Source Quite often in open public areas such as a city park, the local power company may already provide a power box with electrical outlets for private use. This service has to be requested from the power company and a deposit made to secure power costs at the end of the production shoot. The feature producer should search a public area for some sign of a power source facility. It may serve the site survey to make a call to the local power company and request a listing of outdoor power sources.

Clearance/Insurance Needed Personal security for the crew and talent and property damage insurance coverage should be secured before production begins. Academic programs have personal insurance coverage for students and property damage and loss coverage for school equipment, which is active when the shoot is a valid academic project with a supervising faculty member present. Other remote video production projects can easily receive coverage by contacting a reliable insurance agent. Some potential location facilities personnel will require verification of insurance coverage before approval of their location for a shoot. Anticipating insurance notification before facilities personnel require it is a sign of professional competence.

Photographs Taken When more than one location environment is being scouted for a shoot and a decision may be made away from a potential site, an important part of a location site survey is photographs of the proposed location. Instant developing film is most convenient. When adequate photographs of a location site are part of a survey, the photographs help a producer and camera operator plan a shoot and assist a crew after a location strike in restoring a location environment to the arrangement and condition it was before the production crew arrived. The photographs taken should be listed. The photographer's camera position and direction of the lens of the photographed site should be noted on the location diagram as an aid in designing the video camera shots and lens framing.

Traffic Control At some exterior location environments, the extent of a production crew, talent, and equipment will necessitate some control of vehicular traffic. For example, parking restrictions may be required along the area of a shooting set, moving traffic may have to be redirected during a shoot, or a street may have to be closed off entirely from traffic. Most police departments are very cooperative to such requests, but they will need adequate advance notice. In some instances, the approval of a city or town council may be required. This too needs adequate lead time to process the request and get it to the council in time for the shoot or a change of plans if the request should be denied.

Exterior Compass Direction If the remote location is an exterior shoot, an accurate assessment of the compass directions of the area should be made with respect to the proposed shooting site. The sun is the primary light source to an exterior shoot and that source is constantly moving. Knowing the direction the sun takes from east to west on a proposed location is a most important variable to designing an outdoor shoot. A compass is a necessity to scouting a location site. Many location personnel are not accurate about their recollection of east and west directions and are not reliable sources of information for the importance that the sun's direction plays in a remote shoot.

Location Environment Drawing/Map Another important product of location scouting is a drawing or map of the proposed location site. This entails a rough pacing off of the interior and exterior of all environments that are being considered as a location site. Windows should be placed, compass direction indicated, power outlets and circuits noted, and existing furniture and other properties sketched. Everything should be included that may enter into the use of the location from the needs of the production and the adaptability of the location environment.

Other Comments/Observations This area should record any details not covered in the form to this point. It is important to record all impressions of a proposed location site. Sometimes the smallest detail missed or the smallest detail included can become either an obstacle or an asset to the production. When in doubt about including a detail, include it.

- **Production Schedule Form**

Production process Newscast preproduction, feature package preproduction

Responsibility Feature producer

Purpose To organize and schedule the videotape production of individual script and location units of the feature package.

Objective The production schedule form organizes the elements of each remote location into production days and dates for videotaping. The form notifies the production crew and talent of specific location addresses, dates, times, and script pages of scheduling the videotape production of the feature package. The schedule also sets alternate dates, projected equipment set-up and location strike times, and approximate times for completing the shoot.

Glossary

Feature Producer The producer of the feature package is listed here.

Videographer The name of the videographer assigned to the feature producer is listed here.

Package Title The title of the feature package is listed here.

Shooting Day 1 This area of the form sets the specific date—weekday, month, and day—for the first shooting day. The production schedule form also firms up an alternate date.

Location Site The remote location approved for the shoot after the site survey was completed should be noted here. This names the building, geographic area, and address where the videotaping will take place.

Location Map No. This notation relates the location site and address to a municipal map of the geographic area (e.g., H-3).

Location Host The name of the location personnel responsible for the facility or area where the shoot is to occur should be recorded here. This is the everyday contact person with whom the feature producer will cooperate on details of the location and the shoot. A telephone number where the location host can be reached should be included.

Crew Call The time and place of the crew call should be entered here.

Talent Call The time and place for the arrival of talent is listed here. Since the talent do not need lead time for equipment set-up, the talent call can be up to an hour later than the production crew call. Time should be allotted for applying make-up if make-up is required.

Set-up This entry is a range of time including a deadline for the production crew to complete all equipment set-up and checks of the equipment.

Projected Strike This is the approximate termination time for completing the shoot and striking the location.

Shoot Order Units If the preproduction script was arranged in script units, this column records the order in which the script units will be shot.

Script Pages This column records the script pages that will be produced during the shoot.

Setting The specific setting within the location where the videotaping will occur is listed here.

Approx. Time A range of hours and minutes approximating the time needed to complete shooting of the script units or script pages proposed for production during that shooting day.

Cast The talent or cast who will be a part of the videotaping are listed here.

Action Properties On many location shoots, some action properties (e.g., an automobile or an animal) are required. Those action properties required are recorded here beside their respective script units or pages.

Comments The comments section allows the producer the opportunity to make any additional notes to be called to the attention of the crew or talent.

• **Equipment Checklist Form**

Production process Newscast preproduction

Responsibility Videographer, feature producer

Purpose To suggest and account for all possible equipment and accessories necessary for a successful remote video shoot to both the assigned videographer and the feature producer.

Objective The equipment checklist form is an inclusive checklist for equipment and accessories hardware that may be used or needed on a video production location site. The checklist notes, first, the equipment that is available to the production crew, usually the equipment owned by the production facility. Second, the list notes the equipment that may have to be purchased for the shoot. And, third, the checklist allows for notation of any equipment that may have to be rented for the shoot. There are blank lines in the equipment groups to tailor the checklist to a particular production or facility.

Glossary

Feature Producer The name of the feature producer is listed here.

Videographer The assigned videographer responsible for remote videotaping equipment is recorded here.

Location(s) The location(s) for which the equipment will be needed should be noted here.

Package Title The title chosen for the feature package should be entered here. The title may be only a working title at this stage of preproduction.

Date The date the equipment checklist was completed should be entered here.

Avl This abbreviation stands for "available" equipment that may be owned by the news organization. A check in this column indicates that the equipment or accessory is available to the videographer and feature producer and is free to be used on the scheduled production day.

Pch This abbreviation stands for "purchase" and indicates that the needed equipment or accessory will have to be purchased for the production project. Items checked as needing to be purchased will probably require some other requisition step and approval. The checklist also does not imply who will purchase the equipment or when it will be done. The feature producer should follow through on items requiring purchasing.

Rnt This abbreviation stands for "rent" and indicates that the needed equipment or accessory is not available, perhaps too expensive to purchase for the shoot, and will have to be rented from a supplier. Similar to items checked in the purchase column, further steps may be required in the process of obtaining the rented equipment. Some requisition may have to be made, approval received, and rental details made.

Camera/Recorder/Tripod/Test Equipment/Audio/Power Supplies/Lighting/Cables These areas of the form are listed in an attempt to anticipate all possible equipment and accessory needs for a remote video production. Many items may be superfluous. They are listed in an attempt to suggest all possible production needs and equally to suggest the use of some hardware that could be needed during a remote location shoot. One way to use this checklist is to permit it to suggest hardware elements to make the experience of a remote video shoot smooth and productive.

Miscellaneous This area of the form is the result of years of remote video production experience and represents many production disasters during which these elements could have made a difference. Some items are redundant, some may suggest some use not previously anticipated. Most items are helpful to the good order and task facilitation on location.

• **Remote Log Form**

Production process Newscast preproduction, feature package production, news story production

Responsibility Feature producer, reporter/writer

Purpose To record videotaping production details while in the field.

Objective The remote log form facilitates the time-consuming need to view source videotapes after field production in order to note the quality, extent, and content of every videotaped take from the field.

Glossary

Feature Producer The name of the feature producer is listed here.

Reporter/Writer The name of the reporter/writer is listed here.

Videographer The assigned videographer is listed here.

Location The location is the remote site where the videotaping was done.

Package Title The title chosen for the feature package should be entered here. The title may be only a working title at this stage of preproduction.

Location The location at which the videotaping is being done should be entered here.

Date The date the equipment checklist was completed should be entered here.

Page— of This entry permits a record of the total number of remote log sheets and the consecutive numbering of each (e.g., page 1 of 3, page 2 of three, etc.).

VTR Counter/Timer/Code This column records the measure used to clock the length of every videotape take. One method of measuring the length of a videotape take is to read the built-in digital counter on the videotape recorder. Another is to use a stop watch as a timer. Still another is to stripe the source videotape with SMPTE time code and record frames as a measure of the length of a take. Place a check in the correct box to indicate the type of measure used to time the source tape.

Location Since the environment used for videotaping on a location can change (e.g., interior or exterior), this column allows notation of changes within the location for various takes.

Talent Note should be made of the person or persons videotaped during a take. This is a reminder that the full name, correct spelling, and proper title of videotaped talent will be required for character generator copy in postproduction editing or telecast.

Take No. It is not uncommon that more than a single take of any event or interview on location may be videotaped. All takes should be numbered consecutively and the number of each take should be recorded. The number will facilitate recall of the take during editing.

Good/No Good Judgment should be made on location of the various takes during videotaping. Having a recorded comment on the quality of each take as it is completed saves the time of viewing all videotape takes to make the same judgment during postproduction preparation for editing.

Video/Audio Some notation might be made on the video or audio content of each take in this column.

• Talent Release Form

Production process Newscast preproduction, feature package production, news story production

Responsibility Feature producer, reporter/writer

Purpose To give the producer legal rights over the video and audio recording of individual talent.

Objective The talent release form is a legal document that, when filled out and signed by the talent, gives to the feature producer and the news organization the legal right to use the video and audio recording of an individual for publication. This form is necessary in cases of video package content on controversial issues and for underage child talent; however, its use is recommended whenever any talent is being featured in video and audio recording.

Glossary

Talent Name This entry should contain the name of the individual talent recorded on video or audio.

Project Title The title of the video package being recorded is entered here.

Recording Location The location site where the video or audio recording is made should be entered here.

Producer The name of the feature producer should be entered here.

Producing Organization The incorporated name of the video producing organization should be entered here.

Note: The expression, ''For value received'' may imply that some remuneration, even a token remuneration, be required for the form to be legally binding. When there is any doubt about the legal nature of the document, consult a lawyer.

• Editing Work Sheet Form

Note: If adequate and thorough notes were made on the remote log form, completing the editing work sheet may not be necessary.

Production process Newscast preproduction, feature package preproduction, news story preproduction

Responsibility Feature producer, reporter/writer

Purpose To prepare for postproduction editing of the feature package or news story to a master tape from source videotape(s).

Objective The editing work sheet records in videotaping order all video and audio recordings on the source tape. The editing work sheet is a transcription of the source videotape(s). An accurate account of the source video-tape(s) saves a lot of time involved in searching the source videotape(s) during editing. Many postproduction facilities demand this work before access is allowed to editing suites. For the producer and reporter, this stage saves valuable time and cost in postproduction.

Glossary

Feature Producer The name of the feature producer is entered here.

Reporter/Writer The name of the reporter/writer is listed here.

Package Title The title chosen for the feature package or news story slug should be entered here. The title may be only a working title at this stage of preproduction.

Date The date the editing work sheet was completed should be entered here.

Audio: Channel 1/Channel 2 The feature producer or reporter/writer should indicate the correct audio channel or channels and their use on the source tape(s). Since the choice can vary between channels 1 and 2 for field recording, the designation should be made of the channel on which audio recording was made in the field.

Page of This entry permits a record of the total number of editing work sheets and the consecutive numbering of each (e.g., page 1 of 3, page 2 of three, etc.).

Tape No. The number of the videocassette tape being logged should be entered here.

VTR Cntr/Clock/SMPTE Because some measure should be made of the videotape content on the source tape(s), it is helpful to note what that measure is. Choices include the digital counter on the videotape recorder/ playback unit, reading from a stop watch, or reading SMPTE time code. Source videotapes can be striped during videotaping or as a first step in postproduction prior to beginning the editing work sheet. These measures should be consecutive measures made from the (rewound) beginning of the source videotape(s). The VTR counter and stop watch should be set to begin at zero. SMPTE time code is easiest to use when also set to zero at the beginning of striping.

In/Out These columns allow the producer to indicate the beginning and ending measures (VTR counter, clock, or SMPTE) for the particular videotape units being noted.

Notes Any notation about the content of the video or audio on the source tape(s) should be entered here. This is the place to make value judgments about the quality and usability of each take.

Segment Clock Time This column should record the length of time of each particular video or audio bite being noted. Depending on the desired content of any particular video or audio bite, judgment should be made as to whether the time should be from first video to final video or first audio to final audio.

• **Editing Cue Sheet Form**

Production process Newscast preproduction, feature package preproduction, news story preproduction

Responsibility Feature producer, reporter/writer

Purpose To prepare for postproduction editing of the feature package or news story to master tape from source videotape(s).

Objective The editing cue sheet is a postproduction preparatory stage that creates the format and order of edits of the proposed master videotape from the editing work sheet. The editing cue sheet juxtaposes takes from the editing work sheet into the proposed order of edits for postproduction editing. This step permits a lot of creative

work and quality time on the proposed final edited piece without tying up a videotape editing suite.

Glossary

Feature Producer The name of the feature producer is listed here.

Reporter/Writer The name of a reporter/writer is listed here.

Package Title The title of the feature package or the news story slug is entered here.

Date The date on which the editing cue sheet was prepared is entered here.

Audio: Channel 1/Audio: Channel 2 The producer of the package should indicate the correct audio channel or channels and their proposed use on the edited master tape(s). Since the choice can vary between channel 1 or channel 2 and mixed channels, the designation should be made of the channel on which final audio recording will be made.

Page of This entry permits a record of the total number of pages of editing cue sheets for each package or news story and the consecutive number of each page (e.g., page 1 of 3, page 2 of 3, etc.).

Tape No. The number of the videocassette tape being logged should be entered here.

VTR Cntr/Clock/SMPTE Since some measure should be made of the videotape content on the edited master SMPTE tape(s), it is important to note what that measure is. Choices include the digital counter on the videotape recorder/playback unit, the reading from a stop watch, or SMPTE time code. SMPTE time code can be striped on the edited master tape(s) as a first step in postproduction prior to actual editing. These measures should be consecutive measures made from the beginning (rewound) of the master videotape(s). VTR counter and stop watch should be set to begin at zero. SMPTE time code is easiest to use when also set to zero at the beginning of striping.

In/Out These columns allow the producer to indicate the beginning and ending measures (VTR Counter, Clock, SMPTE) for the particular videotape bites being used from the source tape(s) as noted on the editing work sheet.

Notes This space indicates the video and/or IN-CUE audio in-cues and out-cues from the proposed OUT-CUE bites noted on the editing worksheet from the source tape(s). This space will allow the producer to create the proposed edited order of videotape bites from the source tape(s) to the master tape. The in-cues and out-cues may be either video cues or audio cues. Video cues will briefly describe the content of the beginning or end of the bite being considered; audio cues will be the first few words of the beginning of the proposed bite or final few words at the end of the bite being considered.

Segment Clock Time This column should record the real clock time length of each particular video and/or audio bite being proposed. Depending on the desired content of any particular video and/or audio bite, judgment should be made whether the time should be from first video to final video, or first audio to final audio, first audio to final video, etc. When all entries recorded in this column are summed up, the total should approximate the length of the final edited video piece.

- **Edited Master Clipsheet Form**

Production process Newscast preproduction, feature package postproduction, news story postproduction

Responsibility Feature producer, reporter/writer

Purpose To record all character generator copy necessary for the newscast or the edited master feature package or news story.

Objective The edited master clipsheet facilitates for the producer all possible character generator screen text necessary to accompany the edited master videotape for telecast. The form serves as a summary of all essential information not contained on the edited master feature package or news story. This form also serves to prompt the producer to create possible character generator screen text for an edited feature package or news story.

Glossary

Feature Producer This entry lists the producer of the feature package.
Reporter/Writer The name of the reporter/writer is listed here.
Video Editor The assigned video editor is listed here.
Package Title/Story Slug This entry records the title of the news package as proposed on the preproduction forms. This is the title that will label the edited package from this point on.
Audio: Channel 1, 2, Mixed Indication should be made of the final audio channel(s) (1, 2, or both) used for editing. Some producers will edit using both audio channels and expect that the edited master use the mixed audio playback option. Other producers will mix the two audio channels down to either one of the two available channels. The choice made in editing should be indicated.
Length The total edited length of the news package should be timed. Most often, timing is from first audio to final audio. A producer might intend to begin the news package with a video image before first audio begins. This is the point where that choice should be indicated.
Out-cue In the broadcast situation where a video piece is to be B-rolled into a longer program, the studio director will need a video or audio out-cue, a description of the intended final video or the final few words of the audio track. This out-cue should be indicated here.
Character Generator Copy This section of the form records for the producer or control room director all the character generator copy for matting on the news package during telecast.
Videotape/Film Credit When a producer uses video or film footage from another source, screen credit may be required. This entry may be as simple as "File Footage" or "Courtesy of ABC-TV," for example.

In : /Out : For every screen of character generator copy, the producer will have to provide real clock time from the beginning of the video package at which the character generator copy is to be matted over the video and when the matte is to be removed (i.e., the length of time to remain on the screen).
Reporter Lower Third This character generator copy gives the name of the reporter or talent whether the reporter or talent is to be seen on screen or just does a voice-over. Examples of reporter/talent lower third are:

JOHN DOE
News at 5:00

and:

JOHN DOE
Reporting

Interviewee/Actuality Lower Third When interviewees appear on screen, character generator copy is expected. An example of an interviewee/actuality lower third is:

REV. JOHN DOE
Pastor

Voice of When an interviewee does not appear on screen or the interview is done over the telephone, the correct form for character generator copy is to indicate that the audience is hearing the voice of the person only. An example of character generator copy for this is:

Voice of
SEN. JOHN P. DOE
(R) Virginia

Transcription Occasionally transcribed text copy has to appear on the screen over the video image. For example, if an interviewee is speaking in a foreign language, if an interviewee has a very heavy accent, or if the audio quality is very poor, a transcription of a portion of the audio track may have to be matted onto the screen over the interview or actuality. A quotation from a book or a number of statistics from a survey may have to be matted on the screen. This is the place to indicate that text copy.
Trade Credit Perhaps some favor or permission adding to the quality of the news package production warrants an on-screen credit. This screen credit is called a trade. This is the place on the form to indicate that text. An example of a trade credit is:

Reporter's clothes
provided by
FOR MEN ONLY

Video Credits Some news operations provide the opportunity to attach individual credits to a news package itself or provide room at the end of a news program for individual package credits. Even if no provision is made on the news program, adding the proper credits to the clipsheet form provides a record of credits for the video package for future reference. An example of video credits for a new video package is:

JOHN DOE

MARY SMITH   Producer

BILL JONES   Camera Operator

                     Videotape Editor

• Graphics Summary Rundown Form

Production process   Newscast preproduction

Responsibility   Graphic artist/producer

Purpose   To provide the graphic artist/producer with a summary list to circulate to production crew who are involved with graphics sources.

Objective   The graphic summary rundown records the number of, the order in the newscast for, and the content of graphics ordered with the graphics request form or the graphic design form.

Glossary

Graphic Artist/Producer   The name of the graphic artist/ producer who is responsible for the graphics for any particular newscast is listed here.

To: News Producer/Telecine Operator/Technical Director/Assistant Director   This form is a routing form to production personnel responsible for graphics during newscast production.

Newscast Date   The date of the newscast for which the graphics are intended is entered here.

Newscast: Morning/Noon/Early/Evening/Late   The graphic artist/producer must indicate for which newscast the graphics are intended.

Newscast Order   This column lists the graphics in the order in which they are intended to appear.

Story Slug/Feature Title   This column lists the story slug identifier or feature package title with which the graphic is identified. This listing will relate directly to the format/rundown sheet for the respective newscast.

Graphics Description   The graphic artist/producer briefly describes the finished graphic to the extent that anyone reading the rundown and seeing the graphic will be able to recognize it.

Screen Position   Many newscast graphics are intended for squeeze frame matte position on the television screen. This column allows some indication of that positioning.

Source   This column tells the production crew from which video production source the graphic originates. Given that graphics may be 35mm slides, frozen video, or some other storing apparatus, this column notes the sources for each graphic.

• Character Generator Copy/Credits Form

Production process   Newscast preproduction

Responsibility   News producer

Purpose   To collect in one form all of the character generator copy for a newscast.

Objective   The character generator copy form is the master list containing all character generator copy to be

entered into the memory of the character generator before newscast production by the production assistant. This master list is exhaustive and contains all of the closing credits for the newscast. Much of the character generator copy is transferred from individual edited master clipsheets from the reporters and feature producers.

Glossary

Date   This is the date of the newscast for which the character generator copy is intended.

Newscast: Morning/Noon/Early/Evening/Late   The particular newscast for which the character generator copy is prepared is indicated here.

Production Assistant   The name of the production assistant whose responsibility it will be to enter the copy into the character generator's memory is listed here.

Videotape Leader   Insofar as most newscasts will be recorded on videotape even if they are telecast live, some academy leader will have to be recorded.

Storyboard Frames   This form includes aspect ratio frames designed to be typed in by the news producer for maximum clarity. The form has to be read by the production assistant. There are plenty of blank frames. Each storyboard frame has three lines in the upper right-hand corner in which to label the contents of the storyboard frame or the character generator screen page.

Record No.   This box should contain the character generator screen page number for screen recall during production.

Segment 1: Opening   The storyboard frames continue for all segments of the newscast. There are some suggested screen pages on the form. These can be used as is or altered for unique newscasts.

Closing Credits   The closing credits pages of the form follow in the style of general character generator copy pages. These frames suggest producers, production crew roles, and general television program credits. They may be used as they are or altered for a unique newscast.

Record No.   Record number boxes are attached to these frames to record the character generator screen page number for recall during production.

• Video Sources Form

Production process   Newscast preproduction

Responsibility   Videotape operator

Purpose   To provide video source origination information for all edited master videotape and film for any newscast to production crew personnel who require that information.

Objective   The video sources form logs for distribution all video and film sources for any newscast to the units of the format and their point of origination during production.

Glossary

Videotape Recorder Operator   The videotape recorder operator is responsible for all video B-roll sources and their assigned origination. The videotape recorder operator's name is listed here.

To: Technical Director/Assistant Director/Telecine Operator/Video Engineer/Audio Director Because there are many production crew members who need the information contained in this form, it is distributed to these crew members.

Newscast Date The date of the newscast for which the video sources are intended is entered here.

Newscast: Morning/Noon/Early/Evening/Late The videotape recorder operator designates the newscast for which the sources are listed.

Newscast Segment This entry indicates the unit of the newscast for which the video is scheduled to be B-rolled.

Story/Feature This column records the slug or title of the news story or feature package video source.

Graphic Source One of the sources of video in a newscast is that for graphics; this column indicates sources for graphics.

cine/ss/vtr# These three possible sources for graphics list points of origination. *Cine* refers to the telecine, *ss* the still store, and *vtr#* the source of a videotape playback deck that will require a number.

B-Roll Source Because most video playback sources will be edited master videotapes, the videotape playback decks will have to be indicated by number.

vtr#/vtr# These columns record the videotape playback deck number assigned for routing to the switcher during production.

Audio Source Because all audio sources are not wedded to videotapes, some indication of audio sources will have to be designated.

vtr#/cart/live These columns cover possible audio sources during production. *Vtr#* means the audio is wedded to the videotape, *cart* means the audio director will have to play a prerecorded cartridge tape to supply the audio, and *live* means that the audio source will be live in the studio.

Record VTR# This column serves to assign the videotape recorder for the newscast if the newscast is being recorded as well as being telecast live.

• Format/Rundown Sheet Form

Production process Newscast production

Responsibility News producer

Purpose To create the form of the newscast for an individual newscast in the ongoing series. The format/rundown form reflects the newscast design and is the result of the design. The format/rundown sheet is a critical document to the studio production crew during production.

Objective Every news item for the newscast being produced, whether a reader, a news video story, or a video package, is placed in its corresponding order in the newscast on the format/rundown sheet. This format/rundown sheet is identical to the newsroom format board that served to construct each newscast throughout the news preparation day. The format/rundown sheet is broken into the segments of the newscast separated by commercial breaks.

Glossary

Newscast Segment A newscast segment is one of a number of units of the newscast each separated by a commercial break.

Story Slug A story slug is a word or two identifier label for each news story. A slug identifier also serves to label feature packages.

Time The time column serves to record the segment time for each news story or video package.

VID The VID (video) column and checklist boxes are used to indicate whether the corresponding news story has videotape as part of the story.

GPH The GPH (graphic) column and checklist boxes are used to indicate that the corresponding news story requires a graphic matte as part of the story.

Audio The audio column consists of three choices and three columns of checklist boxes. The audio column is used to indicate the form of audio source corresponding to each news story.

vo/crt/lve The choices of audio source origination are vo (voice-over), crt (cartridge), or lve (live). Voice-over means the audio is wedded to the videotape source; crt means the audio source is a prerecorded audio cartridge that must be controlled by the audio director during newscast production; lve means the audio source is live in the studio (usually the talent) and picked up by microphones. If the news story begins with a reader from studio talent and continues with voice-over video, then the lve column is checked as well as the vtr column. The lve column can be marked with a number 1 to indicate the first audio source as the newscast comes on that story, and the vo column marked with a 2 to indicate that the second audio source for that story is the voice-over videotape.

Running/Back Time The final columns in the format sheet record both the running and back times for the newscast. This entry is the sum of the segment times already listed in the time column. Running time begins with 00:00 time and runs to the length (e.g., 28:30) of the newscast. The back time column begins with the total time of the newscast (e.g., 28:30), and all segments of a newscast are subtracted until the end time is 00:00. Note that for both times, the length of the commercial breaks is figured in as part of the calculations.

Glossary

Academy leader The academy leader is the first minute of video preceding the content video of a recorded videotape. It consists of 30 seconds of color bars and audio tone, followed by 20 seconds of the slate of the content of the program, then by 10 seconds of black screen, and, finally, by the opening of the videotaped program.

Actuality An actuality is a sound and/or video bite of a news maker or news event.

Ambience Ambience is any background sound(s) (e.g., city traffic or an airplane flyover) in a recording environment.

A-roll An A-roll video is the primary videotape recording source. In a studio production videotape environment, the A-roll is the master videotape of the program. B-roll is the videotape source that is inserted into the A-roll videotape.

Aspect ratio frame An aspect ratio frame is the television screen proportional rectangle drawing, 3 units high by 4 units long. Aspect ratio frames are drawings used in the design of storyboards. (See the video script/storyboard form.)

Audience demographics Audience demographics is the sum of the individual traits of an audience; e.g., age, sex, education, income, race, and religion.

Audio perspective Audio perspective is the perception that longer video shots should have a more distant sound and closer video shots should have a closer sound. Audio perspective attempts to recreate the sound distance perception of real life.

Audio plot Preparing an audio plot is a preproduction task requirement of an audio director, which includes the judgment of type of microphone to record required sound of a production, microphone holder for picking up required sound, and physical placement of a microphone for a videotape shoot. (See the news set audio plot form.)

Audition An audition is the forum in which prospective anchors and reporters try out for an on-air role for a newscast. Auditions can be used for any on-camera talent role. Prospective talent should attend an audition with a vita or résumé of experience, and a black-and-white glossary picture of him- or herself. During auditions, prospective talent may be asked to read a portion of a script, improvise, or characterize a situation or character.

Banter Banter is ad-lib conversation by a news anchor and other newscast talent usually used at breaks or at the end of a newscast.

Bird's eye view A bird's eye view is the point of view of a set looking directly down on the set from above, noting the confines of the set and set properties. The view can also contain the cast and the camera(s).

Bite A bite is a portion of a video or audio recording actuality.

Blocking Blocking is that process by which a director physically moves participants (cast and camera(s)) to differing points within a location or studio set.

Blocking plot Preparing a blocking plot is the preproduction task of a director, which consists of making a bird's eye view drawing of a set or recording environment with major properties indicated. A director indicates with circles where talent will be placed. The circles are combined with arrows to indicate movement of talent. From a blocking plot, a lighting director can create a lighting plot and a camera operator can decide camera set-up and placement. (See the camera blocking plot form.)

Boom microphone A boom microphone is a microphone, usually directional, designed to be mounted and held above the person(s) speaking. A boom microphone must be aimed at the mouth of the speaker and raised and lowered depending on the camera framing of each camera shot. (*See also* Audio perspective.)

Breakdown A breakdown is a preproduction analysis of either a script or a storyboard. It is intended to separate scene elements from the script or storyboard and arrange them in proposed videotaping order. A breakdown is a necessary component to the development of a production schedule. (See the script breakdown form.)

Bridge A bridge is a video or audio segment that connects, often in summary form, one video or audio subject to another.

B-roll A B-roll is a second videotape source needed in videotape production to perform some video effects involving two video sources during videotaping or editing, such as a dissolve or a wipe. The A-roll would be the primary videotape source into which a B-roll source is inserted.

Character generator A character generator is a video effects generator that electronically produces text on a video screen. The text that is recorded in the memory of the character generator is usually used for purposes of matting over a color background or other video image.

Clipsheet A clipsheet is a summary of information about an edited master videotape. Clipsheets list such information as the title of an edited master videotape, the length of edited video, the character generator copy to be matted over the video during the telecast, and the in-cues and out-cues of the video. (See the edited master clipsheet form.)

Composition of a shot The composition of a camera shot indicates the subject and arrangement of a shot as framed in the viewfinder of a camera. It would indicate the person or object to be framed and the degree of the framing (e.g., CU or XLS).

Contingency Contingency is that percentage amount added to a subtotal of estimated costs in budget making. A common contingency amount is 15% (i.e., 15% of the subtotal of estimated budget costs is added to the subtotal itself as a hedge against actual costs).

Continuity Continuity is the flow of edited images and the content details of edited images from shot to shot. Continuity observation entails the close scrutiny of talent, properties, and environment during videotaping to ensure accurate flow of edited images in postproduction.

Contrast ratio Contrast ratio is the proportion of light to dark areas in electronic video images or across lighted areas on a set.

Control track The control track is a flow of electronic impulses recorded on the edge of videotape that serve as synchronization units for accurate videotape editing. They serve the same purpose as do the sprocket holes on film.

Copy Copy refers to any scripted text to be recorded on the audio track of a videotape or in the memory of a character generator for matting on a video image or background.

Copyright Copyright is the legal right of an artist or author to the exclusive control of the artist's or author's original work. Copyrighted material is protected by law, and the public use of such material must always be cleared by a producer from the owner of the copyright.

Credits Credits are those on-screen texts that list the names and roles played or performed by all members of the crew and cast of the production.

Crew call A crew call is the stated time for the rendezvous of the production team members and is usually at a videotaping site.

Cut-away A cut-away is a video of related but extraneous content inserted into the primary video. For example, video images of a hospital operating room (related but extraneous) would serve as a cut-away insert to a video of an interview (primary video material) with a doctor.

Cut-in A cut-in is a video of necessary and motivated video images to be edited into an established or master scene. For example, close-up shots (necessary and motivated) of two people in conversation serve as cut-ins to a long shot (master scene) of the two people walking and talking.

Cyclorama A cyclorama is the ceiling to floor material used as a simple backdrop for some television studio productions. Cycloramas may be made of a black velour to provide a solid black background or a scrim material that may be lighted with any colored light.

Decibel A decibel is a unit of sound that measures the loudness or softness of the sound.

Depth of field Depth of field is that area in front of a camera (e.g., within a studio set) for which the camera lens is in focus and objects are seen as sharply defined. Movement of the camera or talent in and out of the depth of field requires refocusing of the lens.

DVE (Digital Video Effects) DVE or digital video effects labels a series of video effects that take a video frame from some video source (e.g., videotape or 35mm slide) and manipulate it in any number of ways. Some common DVE effects are image rotation, mosaic effects, peel away, etc.

Edited master An edited master is the final editing of a video piece from source tapes.

Editing cue sheet The editing cue sheet is a listing or format of an edited master videotape developed from the editing work sheet. Entries on the editing cue sheet juxtapose take units from the video described on the editing work sheet into the order of the final edited master. The editing cue sheet is a written format of the final edited master tape. (See the editing cue sheet form.)

Editing work sheet The editing work sheet is a set of notes that describe and time the in-cues and out-cues of all video takes on a source videotape. It can be thought of as a transcription of the source tape. Additional information on the editing work sheet should make some judgmental notation on the acceptability of the video and/or audio of each take. The editing work sheet is a sequential listing of every video segment on a source tape. (See the editing work sheet form.)

Endboard/Endslate The endboard or endslate are terms for the slate when a videotaped take is slated at the end of a take instead of at the front. The endboard is used when a take is redone without stopping the camera and recorder. Endboard use often occurs when talent misses a line.

External video signal The external video signal is the control room signal that carries the program or line of the video program. In some studio operations, that signal can be routed to the individual studio cameras and called up by camera operators on their respective cameras. Having access to the external video signal allows camera operators to match the camera framing over their monitors to the camera framing as seen on the monitor of a camera on line.

Final audio Final audio is used to designate the last sound of copy or music in a video piece. It is a designated endpoint to measure the length of time of an edited master video piece. (*See also* First audio.)

Final edit The final edit is the completed master tape of a video project. It is usually referred to in contrast to the rough edit, which is a preliminary videotape editing.

Fine focus Fine focus is the process in which a camera operator slowly refocuses the camera lens during a camera shot. Fine focus may be required when talent or the camera moves toward the limits of the depth of field.

First audio First audio is used to designate the first sound of copy or music in a video piece. It is a designated beginning point to measure the length of time of an edited video piece. (*See also* Final audio.)

Fishpole A fishpole is an extendible holder for a directional microphone. A fishpole, usually handheld, is extended into a set during dialogue for videotaping.

Foldback Foldback is the process of feeding the audio signal of a studio production back into the studio for the convenience of studio personnel and on-camera talent.

Format A format is the listed order or outline of the content of a video product or program. Format is also used to indicate the genre of a television program, e.g., talk show or newscast.

Freelancer A freelancer is a person who works in the film or video field on a production basis as opposed to being a full-time employee. Writers, producers, and directors are examples of freelancers.

Friction Friction, usually pan and tilt friction, refers to the amount of drag that the pan or tilt mechanisms produce in performing their functions. Adequate friction gives a camera operator control of panning and tilting motions.

F-stop The f-stop units, the calibrated units on the aperture of the lens of a camera, determine the amount of light entering the lens and falling on the pickup tubes.

Future files Future files in news producing is the attempt of the news organization to plan ahead on news coverage needs, e.g., the death of a public figure. A future file on a public figure would contain obituary information and perhaps a lifetime tribute.

Gels Gels (gelatin) are filters used in the control of light for videotaping. Gels are used on lighting instruments to filter light or change lighting temperatures and on windows to change the temperature of light entering a videotaping environment.

Graphic A graphic is a television screen content that contains a still image or text. Graphics can be computer generated, created on 35mm slides, typed into the character generator, freeze framed in a still store, or placed on a showcard on a studio graphic stand. Graphics can be created on site at a television facility, contracted out to an art agency, or purchased as a complete set (e.g., television news graphics).

Hard news Hard news is that news event that is most recent and fast breaking. Hard news is distinguished from soft news.

In-cue An in-cue is the beginning point of copy, music, or video screen at which timing of video or audio inserting is to occur. (*See also* Out-cue.)

Insurance coverage Insurance coverage is required for the use of certain people (e.g., underage children or movie stars), facilities (e.g., television studio or remote locations), and properties (e.g., horses or automobiles).

Intercom network An intercom (intercommunication) network is that system of two-way communication through which television production crew members can interface with each other during studio production sessions.

Interviewee An interviewee is the person being interviewed.

Interviewer The interviewer is the person who interviews.

Lead A lead indicates the beginning video and/or audio of a videotape piece. Leads may be created as a voice-over, a stand-up, or with music.

Leader The leader is the beginning portion of audio or videotape that is used to record information about the subsequent video or audio. Most leaders (often called academy leaders) contain the record of the slate and an audio check (e.g., :30 of tone) with a portion of video black before the video content of the recording. Some leaders also contain a portion of the color bars.

Lead-in A lead-in in television news is the script copy used to introduce another; e.g., talent or feature package. The lead-in is usually only a sentence or two in length.

Legal clearance Legal clearance is the process by which recording and reproduction rights are obtained to use copyrighted materials. Legal clearance must be obtained for copyrighted materials (e.g., music, photographs, or film) and for synchronization (putting pictures to copyrighted music).

Lens filter Television camera lenses, studio and ENG, have the capability of producing visual effects by placing various filters over them. An example of a lens filter is the star filter, which refracts light intense spots (e.g., light instruments or light reflections) in the form of a starburst. Colored lens filters are very common.

Levels Levels are those calibrated input units of light, sound, and video that have to be set to record at acceptable degrees of unity and definition for broadcast reproduction.

Lighting design The lighting design is the preproduction stage during which the mood, intensity, and degree of light for a videotape production is created. The lighting design is the responsibility of the lighting director. The lighting design can be done after location scouting is complete. (See the news set lighting plot form.)

Location A location is that environment outside a recording studio in which some videotaping is to be done, often referred to as the remote location or, simply, the remote.

Location log The location log is the record of all videotaping done on location. The log contains notations about each videotaped take during a remote shoot. The location log serves as the editing cue sheet before postproduction editing. (See the remote log form.)

Logging Logging is the term used to indicate the process of keeping the location log. Logging is also used to record continuity details during a videotaped shoot.

Lower third Lower third refers to the television screen text, usually created at the character generator, which is placed in the lower third of the television screen. A very common lower third is a person's name.

Master tape   A master tape is the videotape containing an edited video project.

Matte   A matte is the visual effect that is created at the production switcher in which two video sources are combined without overlapping images (i.e., what is cut out of one is filled with the other).

Mike grip   A mike (microphone) grip is the individual responsible for holding the microphone or a microphone holder during the recording of audio in a studio or on location.

Mixing   Mixing audio tracks in videotape editing is the process of combining two recorded audio tracks into one audio channel. Mixing usually adds music or ambient sound to a track of voice recording.

News beat   A news beat is the long-term specialized assignment of a reporter or producer to one particular area of interest (e.g., in the area of law, medicine, or religion).

Newscast planning conference   The newscast planning conference is the daily meeting of the news director and staff producers to plan the daily television newscast.

Out-cue   An out-cue is the endpoint of copy, music, or video at which timing or video or audio inserting is to end. (*See also* In-cue.)

Pad   Pad (padding) is a term applied in television production whenever some flexible video, audio, black signal, or time may be needed.

Pacing   Pacing is the perception of timing of the audio or video piece. Pacing is not necessarily the actual speed of a production or production elements, but it is the coordinated flow and uniformity of sequencing of all production elements; e.g., music beat, copy rhythm, or video cutting.

Package   Package is the term used for the production of short video pieces. It is synonymous with soft news video production.

Pickup pattern   Pickup pattern designates the sound sensitive area around the head of a microphone. It is the area within which sounds will be heard by the microphone.

Pickup shots   Pickup shots refers to the practice of videotaping additional studio set or location footage beyond scripted units to be used during postproduction editing. Pickup shots often will be used as cut-aways to cover difficult edits or mismatched edits discovered during editing. Pickup shot subject matter could be anything from a close-up of hands to a set table, an unopened door, or an attentive actor.

Platform boom   A platform boom is a large device for holding a microphone and extending it into a set during videotaping. Most platform booms are on wheels, need to be steered when moved, and require at least two operators—one to handle the microphone and the boom on the platform and the other to move the platform.

Plot   A plot is a creative or technical design usually used for blocking talent within sets, designing sound coverage in audio production, designing the lighting pattern on sets, and listing all properties for a teleplay.

Preproduction script   A preproduction script is a copy of a script for a video project that is considered subject to change. A preproduction script should contain sufficient audio and video material on which to judge the substance of the final proposed project.

Production meeting   A production meeting is a gathering of all production personnel to review details of a production.

Production statement   A production statement is a simple, one sentence expression of the goal or objective of a videotape production. The production statement is a constant reminder at all stages of production of exactly what is being accomplished and why.

Production value   A production value is any element or effect that is used when motivated to create an overall impact. Some examples of production values are music, lighting, and special video effects.

Program format   Program format refers to the content and the order of that content in a television program. Format can also refer to the genre of the program; e.g., talk show or newscast.

Prompter   Prompter refers to either the production crew member responsible for coaching talent during production or the hardware used to project the script copy of a production to the front of the television cameras to assist the talent in reading.

Property   Property is the term used for any movable article on a set. Properties can include furniture, lamps, telephone, food, or bicycle. Properties are classed as set, hand, and action.

Proposal   A proposal is the set of preproduction elements used to present the idea and request for a video production. Most proposals require at least a treatment and a budget. A proposal might also contain a preproduction script and a storyboard.

Rack focus   Rack focus is the process of refocusing a camera lens when the camera or talent have moved beyond the depth of field. Rack focus creates a new depth of field when the camera operator zooms a camera lens all the way out, brings the image into focus, and reframes a shot.

Rate card   A rate card is the list of space, hardware, personnel, services, and the cost for production facilities.

Reader   A reader is a news story within a newscast that has no videotape to accompany it. A reader may or may not have a graphic matte to accompany it.

Record button   The record button is a circular red insert plug found on the bottom of most videotape cassettes. Removing the record button serves as a safety check against recording over or erasing previously recorded video. The absence of the record button will allow playback, but not recording.

Roll tape   ''Roll tape'' is the expression used to signal operation of the videotape recorder at the beginning of a take. A location director uses the expression as a sign of the director's intention to videotape a scene.

Rundown   A rundown/format sheet is a listing of the content and order of a television studio program production. A rundown/format sheet contains the names of talent, timing, video and audio sources, and place of commercial breaks.

Script unit A script unit is that section of a script that designates a videotaping portion and is similar to a scene in a larger act. It is any gratuitous unit that a director may define for production purposes. Many professional scripts number all script units consecutively in right and left margins.

Secondary motion Secondary motion refers to those movements in television that occur with the movement of the camera. Secondary movements include pan, tilt, dolly, truck, arc, zoom, pedestal, and boom.

Serendipity syndrome The serendipity syndrome refers to those good and pleasant effects in television production that were unplanned and unexpected.

Shading Shading in video production is the control of the iris of the lens of a camera. It is the process of setting and/or controlling the iris to permit or exclude light from hitting the camera tubes.

Shoot Shoot is a slang term used to describe a videotape production session either on location or in the studio.

Shooting order The shooting order is the order in which feature package script units will be shot and is indicated on the production schedule. Most often, the shooting order is determined by the availability of locations and talent.

Shooting units Shooting units refers to those portions of a television script that are producible in one continuous videotape take. Shooting units in television are similar to short scenes in theater. In feature package production, shooting units are determined by pages of a script or portions of a page.

Shot list The shot list is a form created during preproduction on which a director indicates types and order of shots to be videotaped. A shot list differentiates between master or establishing shots and cut-ins, provides framing instructions, and indicates the duration of each shot by out-cue. Shot lists are location specific, with the shot list for every location beginning with the count of one.

Slate The slate is an audio and video recording device that allows the labeling of the leader of each take. A slate usually records the title of the production, producer and/or director, date, take number, and videotape code. The character generator, a blackboard, or a white show-card can serve as a slate. Slate also indicates the action of recording the slate on the videotape leader.

SMPTE time code SMPTE (Society of Motion Picture and Television Engineers) time code is an electronic signal recorded on a secondary audio track of videotape to assist an editor in accurately creating a videotape edit. SMPTE time code records the hours, minutes, seconds, and frame numbers of elapsed time for each video frame.

Soft news Soft news is that news event that is not necessarily recent or time sensitive. It is referred to as evergreen or timeless.

Sound effects Sound effects are those prerecorded sounds that simulate sounds in the real environment.

They are used to create a lifelike environment in the television studio and for background to a dialogue track in drama production.

Source tape The source tape is any videotape stock used to record video that will later be edited into a larger videotape project. Source tapes are edited onto a master tape.

Spike marks Spike marks are the result of spiking talent or properties during newscast production. A common form of spike marks are colored adhesive dots placed at the blocked positions of anchors.

Spiking Spiking is the process of recording with some form of marking the blocked position of talent, set property, or studio camera.

Stand-by Stand-by is a verbal command that indicates that the director is ready to begin videotaping a location unit. Production and crew respond to a stand-by command with silence and readiness to begin.

Stand-up A stand-up designates the position of a location news reporter when the reporter appears on camera standing in the foreground of the location. A stand-up may be used as a lead, a bridge, or a tag for a video piece.

Stills Stills are photographs or 35mm slides of some product or subject. Stills can be created in video with a freeze frame. Stills are used often in newscast production for the image of graphic matte.

Still store Still store is a function of digitized video hardware to freeze a video image for storage as a graphic or other still screen use.

Stock shots Stock shots are usually exterior scenes used as settings for studio drama and feature package production. Common stock shots include cityscapes, sunsets, and house exteriors. Many stock shots are found in videotape libraries. Some may be shot specifically for a particular production or package.

Storyboard A storyboard is a series of aspect ratio frames on which are sketched the proposed composition and framing of each shot to be videotaped. Storyboard frames are numbered consecutively, and the audio copy associated with each proposed shot is recorded under the frame. Storyboards are considered essential to some video genres (e.g., commercials) and are encouraged as a quality preproduction stage for all genres.

Strike A strike is the final stage of a location shoot when all production equipment is disassembled and packed for removal and the shooting environment is restored to the arrangement and condition found upon the arrival of the production crew.

Striping Striping is the process of recording SMPTE time code or control track on videotape as a measure of videotape control during editing.

Sweetening Sweetening refers to the process by which audio and video signals are cleaned up and clarified electronically in postproduction. Sweetening audio means to filter out background noises such as hums and buzzes.

Synchronization rights Synchronization rights are those legal clearances in which a producer receives the right to use copyrighted music in a videotape production.

Tag   Tag is the term used to describe the technique of a news reporter of summarizing and delivering a closing remark on a videotaped news piece. A tag can be a voice-over, a stand-up, or music.

Take   A take is a single videotape unit from the beginning to the end of recording. A take usually begins with a recording of the slate and ends with a director's call to cut. It is not uncommon to record many takes of an individual unit. Many takes may be required for one shot.

Talent   Talent is the term used to designate any person who appears in front of a camera (e.g., anchors, actors, and extras).

Talent release   A talent release is a signed legal document by which a producer obtains the right to use the image, voice, and talent of a person for publication.

Target audience   Target audience is the designation of that subset of the public for whom a particular video piece is designed. Knowing a target audience permits a producer and director to make calculated choices of production values to attract and hold the interest of the targeted group.

Telecine   The telecine or film chain is the hardware from which film sources are reproduced for telecast. A telecine island is the video source for 35mm and 16mm film sources. The telecine is usually installed in the master control area of a television production facility.

Timing   Timing is the process of recording the length of a video piece from first to final audio. First audio and final audio might be music and not a vocal cue. Some video pieces may have a visual cue at the beginning or end of the piece.

Titling   Titling is the design and production of all of those on-screen visual elements that create the title of a video production.

Trade   A trade is the exchange of some goods by merchants in a broadcast area for television screen acknowledgment. In some ways it is a form of advertisement. The most common trades in newscast production are the clothes and hairstyling for anchors. In addition, the use of automobiles is a source of trades.

Treatment   A treatment is a preproduction stage in which a producer describes a proposed feature package for the purpose of soliciting approval to go into production with the project. The treatment may include a synopsis of a story, the goal and objective of a package, and the audience's need for the production. (See the package treatment form.)

Vectorscope   A vectorscope is an oscilloscope used to set and align the color of images as they are recorded by the videotape recorder.

Video clip level   The video clip level is that calibrated adjustment on the production switcher by which one matted video source is cut into another by altering the white portions against the darker portions of the images until sharp images are achieved. Clip levels have to be set to matte graphics sharply over the shoulder of a news anchor.

Videographer   A videographer is a photographer working in video.

Voice-over   A voice-over is a production technique in which an announcer's voice is heard without the announcer being seen in the video portion. A voice-over is a common technique in news reporting. Leads, bridges, and tags may all be produced as voice-overs.

Wrap   A wrap is the stage of a production when the director indicates that a good take has been videotaped and signals a move to another shot from the shot list. A wrap is distinguished from a strike.

Selected Bibliography

TELEVISION PRODUCTION TEXTS

Armer, A. *Directing Television and Film*. Belmont, CA: Wadsworth Publishing Co., 1986.

Blum, R. A. *Television Writing From Concept to Contract*. Revised edition. New York: Hastings House, 1984.

Blumenthal, H. J. *Television Producing & Directing*. New York: Harper & Row, 1988.

Carlson, V., and Carlson, S. *Professional Lighting Handbook*. Stoneham, MA: Focal Press, 1985.

Fielding, K. *Introduction to Television Production*. New York: Longman, 1990.

Fuller, B., Kanaba, S., and Kanaba, J. *Single Camera Video Production: Techniques, Equipment, and Resources for Producing Quality Video Programs*. Englewood Cliffs, NJ: Prentice Hall, 1982.

Garvey, D., and Rivers, W. *Broadcast Writing*. New York: Longman, 1982.

Hubatka, M. C., Hull, F., and Sanders, R. W. *Sweetening for Film, and TV*. Blue Ridge Summit, PA: TAB Books, 1985.

Huber, D. M. *Audio Production Techniques for Video*. Indianapolis, IN: Howard Sams & Co., 1987.

Kehoe, V. *Technique of the Professional Make-up Artist*. Stoneham, MA: Focal Press, 1985.

Kennedy, T. *Directing the Video Production*. White Plains, NY: Knowledge Industry Publications, Inc., 1988.

Mathias, H., and Patterson, R. *Achieving Photographic Control over the Video Image*. Belmont, CA: Wadsworth Publishing Co., 1985.

McQuillin, L. *The Video Production Guide*. Sante Fe, NM: Video Info, 1983.

Miller, P. *Script Supervising and Film Continuity, Second Edition*. Stoneham, MA: Focal Press, 1990.

Millerson, G. *Video Production Handbook*. Stoneham, MA: Focal Press, 1987.

Nisbett, A. *The Use of Microphones, Second Edition*. Stoneham, MA: Focal Press, 1983.

Schihl, R. J. *Single Camera Video: From Concept to Edited Master*. Stoneham, MA: Focal Press, 1989.

Souter, G. A. *Lighting Techniques for Video Production: The Art of Casting Shadows*. White Plains, NY: Knowledge Industry Publications, Inc., 1987.

Utz, P. *Today's Video: Equipment, Set Up and Production*. Englewood Cliffs, NJ: Prentice Hall, 1987.

Verna, T., and Bode, W. *Live TV: An Inside Look at Directing and Producing*. Stoneham, MA: Focal Press, 1987.

Weise, M. *Film and Video Budgets*. Stoneham, MA: Focal Press, 1980.

Wiegand, I. *Professional Video Production*. White Plains, NY: Knowledge Industry Publications, Inc., 1985.

Zettl, H. *Television Production Handbook*. Belmont, CA: Wadsworth Publishing Co., 1984.

Zettl, H. *Sight, Sound, Motion: Applied Media Aesthetics*. Belmont, CA: Wadsworth Publishing Co., 1990.

TELEVISION NEWS PRODUCTION

Cohler, D. K. *Broadcast Newswriting*. Englewood Cliffs, NJ: Prentice Hall, 1990.

Fang, I. *Television News, Radio News, Fourth Edition*. Minneapolis, MN: Rada Press, 1985.

Goedkoop, R. J. *Inside Local Television News*. Salem, WI: Sheffield Publishing Co., 1988.

Kessler, L., and McDonald, D. *Uncovering the News: A Journalist's Search for Information*. Belmont, CA: Wadsworth Publishing Co., 1987.

Shook, F. *The Process of Electronic News Gathering*. Englewood, CO: Morton Publishing, 1982.

Stephens, M. *Broadcast News, Second Edition*. New York: Rinehart and Winston, 1986.

Tyrell, R. *Work of the Television Journalist, Second Edition*. Stoneham, MA: Focal Press, 1981.

Yoakam, R., and Cremer, C. *ENG: Television News and the New Technology, Second Edition*. New York: Random House, 1989.

Yorke, I. *The Techniques of Television News, Second Edition*. Stoneham, MA: Focal Press, 1978.

Index